RE-HUMANIZE

Phanish Puranam's research in the field of organizational science focuses on how organizations work, and how we can make them work better. He is known for his work using computational methods to study organizations as complex adaptive systems.

Phanish holds the Roland Berger Chair Professorship in Strategy & Organization Design at INSEAD. He leads the 'Organizations and Algorithms' research programme (supported by the Desmarais Fund at INSEAD), which has trained several doctoral students who are themselves now faculty at leading business schools and which involves collaborators from around the world.

He is also an avid reader and writer of *haiku*.

RE-HUMANIZE

HOW TO BUILD HUMAN-CENTRIC
ORGANIZATIONS IN THE AGE
OF ALGORITHMS

Phanish Puranam

**PENGUIN
BUSINESS**

An imprint of Penguin Random House

PENGUIN BUSINESS

Penguin Business is an imprint of the Penguin Random House group of
companies whose addresses can be found at global.penguinrandomhouse.com

Published by Penguin Random House SEA Pte Ltd
40 Penjuru Lane, #03-12, Block 2
Singapore 609216

Penguin
Random House
SEA

First published in Penguin Business by Penguin Random House SEA 2024

ISBN 9789815144123

Typeset in Garamond by MAP Systems, Bangalore, India
Printed at Repro India Limited

www.penguin.sg

MIX
Paper from
responsible sources
FSC® C047271

For
my son, Pranav,
in the hope that he and his generation will design a
better world than we have

(no pressure)

CONTENTS

Chapter 1: What This Book Is About   1

Part I: The Basics

Chapter 2: What Is Changing   19
Chapter 3: What Remains Constant   49

Part II: How Algorithms Change Organizations

Chapter 4: Algorithms and Organizing   81
Chapter 5: Digital Division of Labour   111
Chapter 6: Digital Integration of Effort   137
Chapter 7: Digital (Non)Hierarchy   165

Part III: A Way Forward

Chapter 8: Democratizing Organization Design   189

Acknowledgements   205
Notes   207

Chapter 1

What This Book Is About

Take a minute to ask yourself this: What do you see when you try to imagine the organizations you might be working in a decade from today?

You might imagine things that fill you with delight. We have finally surmounted the pains of digital transformation that were so widespread a decade ago. Humans use sophisticated artificial intelligence (AI) to enhance their thinking and creativity as naturally as we use our smartphones today. Data-driven decision-making is the norm. The obligatory daily commutes and business travel for 'face time' with clients and bosses are gone (and so is the associated damage to the environment); we collaborate in the metaverse as much as we do face-to-face, and we are free to choose which one we prefer.

Our colleagues come from all over the world and represent the full diversity of the workforce. Most work is bespoke, interesting, and meaningful; automation can take care of the rest that is not. We form teams to tackle projects that are led by individuals who enjoy our respect and trust. Organizations are smaller, and the multilayered command and control hierarchy is gone, along with all its pathologies of inequality and red tape. Most importantly, we get a wage we consider fair, and the work we do gives us a sense of purpose; our organizations feel like communities that we appreciate belonging to. In short, the digitalization of organizations is complete, and humankind has won.

Or you might imagine things that fill you with dread. Organizations have become collections of remotely located individuals who never meet, only interact digitally, and look puzzled at the concept of the workplace as a community. Going to work feels oppressive; we are surveilled, measured, and manipulated to unbearable levels based on the mountains of data now available. We may look superficially diverse, but the reality is that every colleague has been through the same algorithmic screen to fit with the organization's goals. We really work in culturally homogenous hives.

Our hierarchies may be flatter, but they are flat only in layers, with intolerable and intrusive levels of control and supervision by a few algorithm-assisted super-managers. Meaning, purpose, and community? We seek those, if we can, in virtual realities outside the workplace. The worst of these scenarios involve a techno-elite, controlling organizations made up of algorithms that make today's smart contracts look like a joke; the few remaining human employees only perform tasks that require hard-to-automate manual dexterity or fulfil some legal requirements. The rest struggle with the constant fear of unemployment. In short, the digitalization of organizations is complete, and the algorithms have won.

Neither of the futures outlined above (or their combinations) is guaranteed to materialize. But what we choose to do today as the designers of organizations will matter in shaping what is to come. This is true if you are building a new organization today—a start-up, a new team or division within an established company, a new agency in a government, or an international organization like the United Nations or the World Bank. But it is also true if you want the organization that you already are in today to have a viable future, regardless of whether it is in manufacturing or services, in the 'new' or 'old' economy, in the public or private sector.

Our choices about organization design will matter for the future of organizations.

The Problem

Almost nothing we have accomplished as a species, good or bad, would have been possible without organizations. I do not only mean corporate, military, or government hierarchies. In the history of our species these are very recent, and, possibly, transient forms of organization. Rather, by 'organization' I simply mean a group with a goal—a system that typically allows people to collectively achieve what no individual could. As Yuval Noah Harari put it quite memorably, one on one, our superior minds would be of little use in a conflict with a chimpanzee, our closest cousin in evolutionary terms. Collectively, by organizing ourselves, we control the planet; some of us even worry about conserving chimpanzee habitats.[1]

Put simply, **our species is dominant on this planet because our superpower is the ability to organize ourselves in flexible ways to pursue a variety of goals**. Every cultural institution and technology we are proud of owes its origins to it. How this superpower could be affected by rapid developments in digitalization—the incorporation of digital algorithms into the fabric of organizations—is the theme of this book.

My basic premise is that organizations have been essential to humankind's journey, but digitalization makes their future look uncertain. The reason is that the technologies associated with digitalization, specifically algorithms of varying degrees of intelligence, appear likely to worsen a problem that existed long before they did. This problem has to do with the tension between two quite distinct roles that organizations fulfil in our societies.

First, organizations are systems for collectively attaining what is individually impossible. The term 'organization' derives from the Greek root for the word 'tool', and this is in keeping with our thinking about them as instruments that help us accomplish goals. When organizations fulfil this function effectively, we say they are **goal-centric**.

Second, organizations are also communities of connection, meaning, and shared purpose, the natural habitat of *homo sapiens*. Belonging to organizations is an important way in which we express our humanity as a group-living species. When organizations fulfil this function effectively, we say they are **human-centric**. Organization designs optimized for goal centricity may or may not be very human-centric, and vice versa.

We should care about human centricity, as I explain at length in this book, for at least two reasons. The first reason is that we might care about human welfare for its own sake. For many, including me, this is enough reason. But I do draw a salary from a business school, so I will also offer a second reason: human centricity aids goal centricity by producing motivation.

When I told my colleagues that my new book was about keeping organizations human-centric in the age of algorithms, some reacted with a wry 'they are hardly human-centric now!' I acknowledge that organizations today already face considerable challenges in pursuing goal centricity while remaining human-centric. I trace these difficulties to three features of modern organizations that reinforce each other: scale, specialization, and centralization (whether it is coupled with the logic of shareholder value maximization or not).[2] I believe that digitalization could make things much worse, in ways I'll describe in detail. On the other hand, digitalization could also improve the human centricity of organizations, if we have the wisdom to choose well in how we adopt it.

Others wondered if I was falling for the hype. It does seem a bit strange to worry about the digital future of organizations when many of them are still struggling today to simply digitize their data and processes, or pool different kinds of data. But digitalization, much like a pandemic, is a network-driven phenomenon: Slow starts can blind us to the possibility of explosive growth. The future has surprised us before with how quickly it arrived and how unprepared we were for it. Those who ride the wave of overenthusiasm don't look any more foolish than those who are caught with their head in the sand when things change rapidly.

'So, what's new?' some others have asked me. After all, technologies have been changing how organizations work for a long time, destroying some jobs, creating others, changing how humans solve problems and collaborate, and how bosses manage.

A major part of the answer to the 'what's new' question is the scale, scope, and speed of technological change occurring today. In particular, the rapidity of development of algorithms that do what only humans formerly did inside organizations—namely take decisions, coordinate actions, and monitor and persuade each other—has been breathtaking. I am talking, of course, about AI. Wherever in the digital transformation journey an organization is today, I am convinced that AI is an important destination ahead, if not the final one, and it will occupy a large share of our attention going forward.

While the field of AI has been around for a while and has had many slow periods ('AI winters'), there has been rapid progress since the Deep Learning Revolution took off around 2012. The rate of change is a matter of degree, but in this case, the degree is enormous. Military strategists have a saying: Beyond a certain level, quantity has a quality of its own. Complexity theorists use the phrase 'more *is* different'. In other words, when some thresholds are crossed, the very nature of the change can be transformative.

How we organize, in the very practical sense of how we hire, retain, motivate, train, decide, collaborate, and implement, all can change very rapidly as digital transformation unfolds and paves the way for widespread AI adoption. **Whether AI and other digital technologies are disruptive to companies or not, we should**

take seriously the possibility that they will be disruptive to the people inside them.

The second important part of the answer is that in addition to being *tools*, as earlier generations of technologies typically were, AI algorithms now can also take on the roles of teammates. AI colleagues who act with a fair degree of autonomy are rapidly becoming a widespread reality. They create new opportunities for gains from collaboration, but also new forms of dependence, competition, and obsolescence for humans.

To be clear, I am not concerned about 'rogue robots'. We don't need algorithms to become sentient and evil (if either is ever possible) to start worrying about their effects on organizations. Rather, my point is that ceding the role of teammate to these technologies can fundamentally affect the ways in which we humans interact and organize ourselves, *even if* the AIs are fully aligned to the interests of the humans they work for (and even with). Recognizing these changes is vital to prevent undesirable shifts that may be hard to reverse. This can also offer opportunities to improve how we organize ourselves relative to how we do it today.

The problem this book addresses can be stated succinctly as follows: Instead of being passive observers of inexorable trends, **how can we actively manage digitalization to attain both goal and human centricity in our organizations?** It's a problem relevant to anybody who expects to work in and lead organizations of any size and form—from small teams to online communities, governments, and mega-corporations.

That's pretty much everybody.

Why Solving It Is Important

Even if you grant that organizations may be at greater risk than ever of losing their human centricity as they undergo digitalization, you might ask why that means we should do something about it. Here are three kinds of arguments I've heard—all of which say we shouldn't—and why I find none of them persuasive.

Let's dispose of the minor one first, which could be stated as follows: If organizations are efficient at generating value and can pay their members enough, won't these members simply take the cash and accept a less human-centric work context? Perhaps they could seek community, purpose, 'and all the other good stuff' elsewhere? Isn't this what's already happening?

I think this is a myopic viewpoint in a world in which intrinsic motivation is valuable and human-centric organizing can generate it. As every manager comes to recognize, pay and other forms of material benefits are important but hardly sufficient to get an organization's members to work their collective magic. Unless you can also offer a social context that they value and want to belong to, you are likely to be dealing with a collection of sullen individuals bound together only by a pay cheque, doing the bare minimum you can monitor and coerce them into doing, and looking for the first chance to exit. The fact that many organizations are failing to accomplish human centricity today does not invalidate the claim that there is value in being human-centric.

A second argument can be stated along these lines: If digitalization is complete, there may be no need for human workers and organizations at all. AI (and other digital technologies) will do everything, and humans may not have to work any more to earn a living. Let's call this scenario 'zero-human organizing'. In this case, why bother with trying to create human-centric organizations?

This argument does usefully remind us that a necessary condition for the human centricity of organizations is that they contain at least some humans! But it also has problems. The timeline for when zero-human organizing will be widespread is uncertain at best; it may never happen at all. Even if unemployment spikes due to automation, I believe there will be people alongside digital algorithms inside organizations for a long time to come, because not everything can be easily automated, nor will be worth automating. The near future for organizations is therefore a bionic one—infused with digital algorithms, but not without humans (more details in Chapter 2).

Given how poor most governments are today in terms of effective redistribution of wealth, I am inclined to view the talk about a leisure-filled world with Universal Basic Income as a form of utopian (social) science fiction. But even if a world without the need to work arrives, we should not overlook the fact that organizations are the natural habitat for humans as a group-living species. Surveys show that very few people (3 per cent) think they would stop going to work if a basic income was provided—though respondents think most other respondents (52 per cent) would stop! Across trials, most people show no change in hours worked, nor do they drop out (or into) the workforce if they receive guaranteed basic income.[3]

Let me interpret this in organizational terms: Paraphrasing Voltaire's famous quip about God, we might say that even if no economic reason to form organizations existed, human nature will very likely compel us to form organizations to pursue other goals, such as exploration or creativity. Organization design in this future might look a lot like multiplayer video game design does today. Making organizations human-centric will become more, not less, important.[4]

The third and, in my view, most serious challenge to my objectives pertains to defining what human centricity really is. If we are talking about ensuring that organizations offer what humans value (besides pay), what are these attributes? And which humans are we talking about? What, if anything, is universally true about what humans want from the organizations they belong to? How do we know these won't change over time? Given the enormous variation across cultures and demographics, isn't it foolhardy to even attempt to define human centricity?

These are hard questions, but we cannot duck them. Anthropologist Robin Fox once noted, 'We could not plead against inhuman tyrannies if we did not know what is inhuman.'[5] If we take the stance that nothing universal can be said about what we value in the organizations we belong to, the risk is that we will fail to take a collective stance against the applications of algorithmic technologies in a manner that will end up dehumanizing organizations for all of us. Surely, an attempt is worthwhile, and this is the first goal for this book. I offer my attempt at defining human-centric organizing in a rigorous manner based on the concept of organizational context preferences (Chapter 3).

I believe that algorithmic exploitation and zero-human organizing are not the only possible futures. This book offers the thesis that with thoughtful adoption, algorithmic technologies could in fact be used to increase rather than decrease human centricity in organizations while also enhancing goal centricity. Once we define clearly what human centricity is, I will argue that digital technologies can be deployed in ways that older technologies could not, to help create organizations that are both goal- and human-centric. Developing a vision, if not a blueprint, for this approach is the second goal for this book.

What I Hope to Contribute to Solving It

While many of the challenges of digital technologies to human centricity occur also in society at large, we are a group-living species, and it is at the organizational level I believe we have the best chances of confronting and overcoming these challenges. It is also where we will need to conduct experiments—lots of them—to find ideas that can be scaled up to societies.

I've spent two decades studying organizations. During this period, researchers have made substantial progress in the field of organization design, which is the branch of organization science concerned with the study of how organizations work and how we can make them work better. I've been fortunate to be a part of the action, directly through my own research as well as indirectly through that of my graduate students and colleagues.

As a founding member of some of the academic communities and think tanks that led the rapid pace of developments in organization design research, I have had a ringside view of some of the best thinking in this domain. Our collective body of work gives us useful frameworks and results to begin rethinking what organizations might look like in the not-too-distant future.

'The Future of Work' is the label often applied to a range of conversations we are having in organizations today about technology, about diversity and inclusion, about remote working, about working from home—and the consequences of all these things. These are important conversations, but I have found them to be rather disjointed. I'm going to propose that we change the conversation to be about the 'future of organizations'. The reason is that ultimately what humans do collectively— for work or entertainment—is going to be performed in some kind of organization. These might be distributed, they might be decentralized, they might be digital, and hopefully they will be highly diverse. But they will be organizations.

Therefore, the future of work is essentially the future of organizations, and organization design thinking offers a perspective that integrates these disparate threads. I believe that ideas about organization design can help us to proactively shape the impact of digital transformation on organizations rather than passively react to trends that seem unstoppable. I've had opportunities to validate this belief in my consulting and teaching, in leading workshops and conversations with leaders of corporations, government agencies, start-ups, NGOs, and international organizations like the UN.

I recognize there are many well-established ways of thinking about organization design. We have the pioneering work of Jay Galbraith (the Star Model), David Nadler and Michael Tushman (the Nadler-Tushman Congruence Model), Tom Peters and Robert Waterman (the McKinsey 7S Framework), and Richard Burton and Børge Obel (multi-contingency theory). We also have more recent thinking about the importance of human centricity in organizations by Frederic Laloux, Gary Hamel, and Michele Zanini, and more and less critical views on their thoughts from Nicolai Foss, Peter Klein, and Markus Reitzig.[6]

I have read and learnt from all of them. I'd like to let readers make up their own minds as to what is unique and useful about the approach I describe here vis-à-vis these fellow travellers—all of us care ultimately about improving how organizations work. The organizational challenges posed by digitalization that I describe here are so complex that a diversity of perspectives on them is surely desirable.

Consider this book my contribution to that diversity.

The Rest of This Book

I have divided the book into three parts to help make the logic of my arguments as clear as possible. The first section covers my basic assumptions about what is changing in organizations and what will not. The second section goes in detail about how digital algorithms can change each aspect of how we organize, in both undesirable and desirable ways. The last section concludes with an (unabashedly optimistic) vision of how we could rethink the process of organization design to explicitly balance human and goal centricity.

In more detail:

The next section is **The Basics**. It has two chapters.

Chapter 2: What Is Changing

This chapter unpacks the triad of mutually reinforcing forces that are driving the digitalization of organizations: connection, representation, and aggregation. I will explain why digitalization also underpins other major organizational trends such as remote working, decentralization, and even diversity and inclusion. Central to digitalization itself is AI, which enhances decision-making by identifying patterns in data and predicting outcomes. I outline the challenges and opportunities (discussed in detail in the rest of the book) that technologies like AI pose for keeping our organizations human-centric, even as they are rapidly becoming 'bionic'—infused with digital technologies.

Chapter 3: What Remains Constant

In this chapter, I introduce the concept of organizational context preferences (OCPs) and their importance in designing human-centric organizations. I argue that while digitalization transforms many aspects of work, the basic structure of human preferences for autonomy, relatedness, competence, fairness, collective purpose, and novelty in organizational contexts remain constant. This is a strong claim, but one that I make based on an extensive review of the literature, and my own analyses.

These preferences are deeply rooted in our evolutionary history as a group-living species and are crucial for intrinsic motivation, though cultural and individual differences can lead to vastly different weights on them. The chapter emphasizes that satisfying OCPs not only enhances employee well-being and satisfaction but also contributes to goal centricity by fostering intrinsic motivation, reducing supervision and costs, and improving an organization's ability to compete for talent. The OCPs thus offer a touchstone for testing whether any new technology we adopt will decrease, preserve, or increase the human centricity of our organizations.

The next section is called **How Algorithms Change Organizations**.

Chapter 4: Algorithms and Organizing

To understand how digital algorithms change organizations, it is useful to first develop a clear picture of how organizations do what they do—namely how they enable groups to achieve goals. I will introduce the universal problem of organizing or UPO framework. Unlike many other approaches to organization design that list bundles of possible instruments and solutions (e.g., structure, skills, culture, systems), this approach focuses on the problems of organizing that are universal, and that matter regardless of the scale, sector, or history of an organization. These problems pertain to division of labour, integration of effort, and handling exceptions and conflicts arising from imperfect solutions and the need to adapt to changing conditions. Designing an organization entails finding solutions for these problems that are feasible and effective in particular contexts. A design is a context-specific set of solutions to these universal problems. I also discuss the use of data and algorithms to improve organization designs.

Chapter 5: Digital Division of Labour

Every organization has a division of labour, and specialization, while common, is not the only possible approach. High levels of specialization can boost efficiency but often detract from the human-centric aspects of work, such as meaning, novelty, and autonomy. It can de-skill people in harmful ways. Digital algorithms risk amplifying these negative effects, creating hyper-specialized and monotonous tasks, and de-skilling individuals as they succumb to the lure of convenience. However, algorithms can also be used to design divisions of labour that respect the organizational context preferences or OCPs, fostering both human and goal centricity. I introduce the logic of 'ensembling' as a form of human–AI collaboration that avoids many of the negative aspects of specialization.

Chapter 6: Digital Integration of Effort

I argue that the ability to effectively integrate efforts at a large scale relies ultimately on techniques to prune and smooth interactions (to prevent conflicts) and absorb the conflicts that remain. This chapter focuses on pruning and smoothing to avoid conflicts, the next focuses on absorbing and resolving conflicts. Historically, cultural beliefs, standards, and procedures to compartmentalize work have enabled large-scale integration of effort. Today, digital technologies like AI algorithms, blockchain, and remote work platforms offer new ways to achieve pruning and smoothing. However, it is crucial to ensure these technologies align with OCPs to foster human-centric work environments.

Chapter 7: Digital (Non)Hierarchy

In this chapter, I contrast two organizational paradigms enabled by digital technologies: the panopticon and the collaboratory. The panopticon uses surveillance and centralized control to absorb conflicts and manage large groups with minimal effort at supervision. It leads however to a loss of autonomy and increased power imbalance. In contrast, the collaboratory, a concept rooted in peer-to-peer collaboration and decentralization, leverages digital tools for smoothing and pruning interactions to enable groups to manage themselves. While the panopticon symbolizes coercive oversight, the collaboratory represents a human-centric approach that empowers individuals and enhances collective problem-solving. Which one we will build is up to us.

The final section of the book, **A Way Forward**, ends with a vision for how we might go about designing organizations in the age of algorithms.

Chapter 8: Democratizing Organization Design

In this last chapter, I describe an approach to organization design that I believe is suitable for the challenge of balancing human and goal centricity as organizations continue to absorb advanced digital algorithms—wisely, I hope. This approach is called 'decentralized designing' and is characterized by three key pillars: 1) allowing for diversity in designs across sub-units; 2) ensuring local participation in the formation of designs to leverage local knowledge and foster motivation; and 3) utilizing AI algorithms and data to support participative design and ensure global coherence of the resulting designs. I can't claim that decentralized designing is entirely new or a panacea, but I do claim that it can be useful in the journey ahead for organizations.

In sum, I take the point of view in this book that organizations exist to serve us, not the other way around, and that they serve us best by being both goal-centric and human-centric. Balancing both has always been hard, but digitalization will make it harder. However, I believe it is possible, once we can recognize this risk, to navigate digitalization and the adoption of AI technologies in a way that improves the goal centricity of organizations while preserving or enhancing their human centricity.

PART I

THE BASICS

Chapter 2

What Is Changing

Between 2003 and 2024, the maximum number of data points used to train a cutting-edge artificial intelligence (AI) algorithm increased from about 500 million to 15 trillion. In the same period, the maximum number of parameters in the leading models increased from 120 million to 1.6 trillion and the computation needed to train those models increased from 1 petaflop to 50 billion petaflops.

These monstrous, hard to visualize numbers tell a story about the relentless pace of digitalization and where it points, that words alone cannot. Think about the incentives and the intense competition that drive the collection of vast datasets, the investments in R&D needed to develop complicated algorithms with huge number of parameters, and the investments in software and hardware that produced the raw computation power that allows us to extract insight from these data points.

You don't need to know what a petaflop is (hint: it's not a movie about dogs that turned out to be a box office disaster) to notice that while the amount of data used to train these models has only increased by 30,000 times (!), the amount of computation we now use to extract insight from that data has increased by 50 billion times. Roughly speaking, we are throwing about 1.7 million times more computation at each data point than what we were doing twenty years ago. These numbers have probably increased dramatically in the time between this manuscript leaving my hands and arriving in yours via my publisher. The trends may eventually flatten out, but right now they look like rocket ships taking off when you graph them.[7]

Ask yourself why this is happening, who hopes to gain what by it, and what might come of it, and you might glimpse the tectonic forces that are driving digitalization in our societies and organizations. You might also see why the digitalization journey for most organizations, even if it begins with something as prosaic as digital invoicing or implementing an enterprise resource planning or ERP system, will likely lead towards artificial intelligence algorithms into nearly everything they do.[8] And you might begin asking yourself what sort of a role humans will have in the organizations of the future, and the timeline over which we can say something meaningful.

Digitalization is also a useful lens through which we can understand other important trends that are affecting organizations, such as distributed working, decentralization, and the growing importance of managing diversity (of demographics and attitudes). Together with digitalization, they constitute the '4Ds' of what's changing for organizations. I believe it's useful to see each of these through the prism of digitalization because I believe all of them are intricately intertwined with the digital technologies that we use, and with AI.

To be sure, there are technologies beside AI that are emblematic of the forces of digitalization today—cloud computing, Web 3.0, virtual/augmented reality, blockchain, and quantum computing. But rather than talk about any specific technology (the exact list might well look quite different five years from today), I want to discuss a set of basic processes that underlie digitalization. These are general, and they help understand what digitalization is doing to so many aspects of organizational life.

Beyond that, I want to explain why I think AI is *the* digital technology to which all others converge or at least connect, in one form or another—it's the one ring to bind them all, and the one that I believe will have the strongest impact on how we organize. This, I will argue, is because the value from extracting intelligence from data that digitalization enables is just too enormous to ignore, and AI is what makes that possible. It is also becoming a serious competitor to humans in that role, and I will discuss some possible futures towards the end of this chapter.

Digitalization as Representation, Connection, and Aggregation

Nobody thinks of gramophone records when thinking of digitalization. I mean those circular black clay discs that nestled inside glossy magazine-like sleeves. Do you even know what I am referring to? People of a certain vintage (and some nostalgia buffs) will. There's something magical about dropping the needle gently onto a spinning disc, hearing the pops and hisses and then have it miraculously turn into music. These vinyl-based records represented music as physical grooves. As the needle traversed the groves, the bumps it encountered gave rise to vibrations that could be converted into sound. Voilà! Recorded music. These came to be called LP or long-playing records, which ran on for the amazing duration of forty-five minutes, before you had to pick them up, flip them over, and play the other side.

Eventually (I'm skipping over magnetic tapes) came the era of the compact disc (CD) with music digitally encoded as zeroes and ones. Music had moved from being grooves in a physical medium to being represented as bits in a digital medium. But what good were CDs if we couldn't share music easily? Enter Napster and iTunes. Music files exchanged in a giant web of peer-to-peer sharing. Suddenly we could get hold of that obscure single from a fan in Tokyo.

And then came Spotify. Aggregating all those MP3s into one big database and running clever algorithms to figure out which songs are similar to the ones we had heard and liked. Spotify can now answer questions such as which songs you are more likely to enjoy, what are your friends listening to and liking, which song is more likely to be successful and downloaded many times, using that aggregated data. This is what you can do once you have all this aggregated data together in one place through the application of algorithms that can extract intelligence out of data.

These three processes—representation, connection, and aggregation—form a loop of mutually reinforcing processes that underlie digitalization (Figure 1).[9] Once the loop gets going in any field of activity, the returns to strengthening each element pull in more investment, which in turn makes investment in the other two elements even more attractive, and so on. Investments in digital representation, connectivity, and aggregation are what economists call complements—investment in one increases the value of investing in the other.

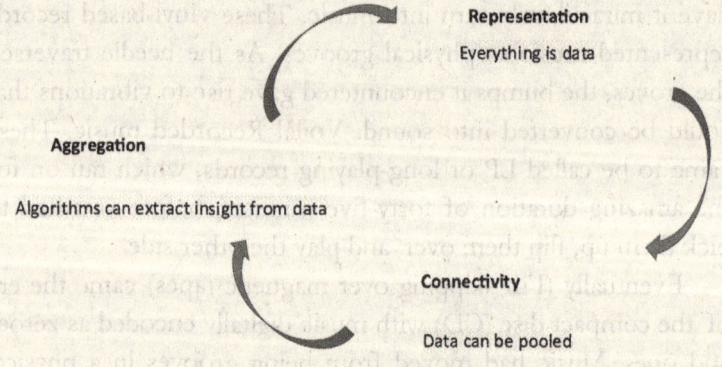

Representation
Everything is data

Aggregation
Algorithms can extract insight from data

Connectivity
Data can be pooled

Figure 1: The basic processes of digitalization

Let's consider each in some more detail. First, there's digital representation—the conversion of things that are in the physical world into digital format. The movement from music in the form of physically recorded grooves on vinyl record into strings of bits in a digital medium is one example, but so is the conversion of paper invoices and ledgers into digital records. The explosion of sensor technologies, which can record an enormous variety of real-world processes such as the movement of cars and pedestrians, temperature and wind speeds, ambient sound, or even the faces of individuals as they go about their daily work, has in turn exploded what can be digitally represented.

So many of our activities in the real world today are mediated by digital technologies. Between your phone, laptop, tablet, computer, VR headset, and smartwatch, there is little about your life that does not get digitized. Try this exercise for yourself: Keep track of the number of hours in a day that your activities leave a digital imprint in some system. (If you wear a smartwatch, the answer is easy to compute—it is twenty-four hours). In principle, there are very few things left that we do in the real world that would not, almost by default, leave a digital trace unless we took explicit steps to prevent that from happening. Digital representation means that everything that can be observed is (potentially) data.

All that explosion in data brought about by digital representation by itself would be worth nothing if someone could not extract something useful from it. Connectivity is essential for that. I mean connectivity between the producers and analysers of data as well as between multiple producers of data that can then be pooled. Connectivity is shaped by the shape of networks. This is why networks between people, between people and machines, and between machines themselves (nowadays called, somewhat ominously, the Internet of Things or IoT) are the backbone of digitalization. Connectivity allows data to be pooled.

Finally, all that pooled data has to be aggregated into something useful. The synthesis of insight from the pool of data is critical to do anything useful with it. The synthesis could be in human minds, or in statistical analysis algorithms, or increasingly in artificial intelligence algorithms. Aggregation produces value from data.

Representation, connectivity, and aggregation are the three basic processes underlying digitalization, and they also help understand how every digital technology that we talk about today is transforming organizations.

What's cloud computing? It's a technology that quite literally aggregates and connects digitally represented information in a distributed system that can be used from anywhere in the world, and at much lower storage and processing costs compared to each organization creating its own storage.

What are blockchains? These are a particular way of representing digital transactions, connecting them up across people, and aggregating them in the form of something called a distributed ledger that creates an immutable record of these transactions. The records can't (easily) be hacked and they can't be changed any more. This capacity to create immutable records is the real power of blockchain. I have no idea if crypto currencies will ever replace fiat money (the kind backed by a central bank, such as dollars and pounds), but I am reasonably sure blockchains and distributed ledgers will become ever more useful for managing supply chains and even perhaps establishing the provenance of digital content, to avoid deepfakes and other kinds of digital forgery.

How about virtual/augmented realities and the metaverse? This refers to a set of technologies that allow us to convert our analogue physical selves into a digital representation using avatars that can then connect with each other. There is no connectivity without digital representation in the metaverse. The next step would be to take all the data from that connectivity and design better interactive experiences for us through aggregation, and this is undoubtedly where the industry is going.

Each of these technological trajectories is driven by the same underlying set of basic processes around digital representation, connectivity, aggregation, and the next step for many is the extraction of insight from that aggregation. This loop of digitalization has been playing out across a variety of industries, not just the music industry, and it is also fundamental to understanding the impact of other major trends affecting organizations today.

Digitalization Catalyses Other Trends in Organizing

Digitalization is certainly not the only thing that is changing about organizations today. However, I believe that a focus on digitalization is appropriate because it is the lens through which all other changes are filtered in terms of their consequences for organizations. Let's consider three other important changes that also dominate the 'future of work' conversation today, and why digitalization is critical to understand the implications of each.

First, there is the explosion in **geographically distributed work** (aka remote working, working from home, hybrid work). This is not a novel idea; people have been collaborating across geographic distances for centuries, and for profit at least since the days of the notorious East India Companies (British and Dutch). The offshore outsourcing of services that boomed in the first decade of this millennium saw the emergence of sophisticated organizational models to stitch together the work of coders, back-office processing staff, and eventually even R&D teams that were located halfway across the world. Open-source software online communities have been working in a distributed fashion for decades. Working for some days from home and for some organizations working entirely remotely was already a fact of life even before December 2019.

However, what has brought this concept home for all of us is the covid-19 pandemic. Before, many of us believed that certain tasks could only be accomplished through in-person interaction. While this is still true for many activities, we have come to realize that there are numerous tasks that do not require physical co-presence, in large part because technologies for digital collaboration and organizing are surprisingly effective for many things.[10] In the early days of the pandemic, there was this meme going around that I found exquisitely funny. It was framed as a multiple-choice question:

Q: Who's had the biggest impact on digital transformation in your company?

1. the CEO
2. the CTO/CIO
3. the board
4. covid-19

And the correct answer, of course, is covid-19. Objectively, there were no radically new digital technologies that became widely available to organizations between December 2019 and March 2020. What happened instead was the adoption or rather scaled-up utilization of several pre-existing technologies like Dropbox, Zoom, Slack, Teams, and Google Docs to help us connect and work better together, given that we were all now forced to do so in a distributed fashion. What changed was necessity, urgency, and mindset. All the digital tools were already there.

A second transformative trend is the emphasis on **diversity and inclusion**. This issue has been simmering in the background for quite some time, but social and regulatory pressures in many parts of the world are compelling leaders to provide a clear account of their efforts to enhance diversity. But for diversity to be more than just a slogan or an ideology, we need the data and analytics that digitalization provides.

In 2022, many companies in the UK were celebrating International Women's Day by tweeting hyperbole about their fantastic support for female colleagues. However, in the UK, salary data is public. Some clever hackers developed a bot that identified and exposed the gender pay disparities in companies that were boasting about their achievements on the diversity and inclusion front.[11] Right next to the CEO's self-congratulatory tweet, the bot would tweet the gender pay gap in that company!

Inclusion is another theme related to diversity and equity, and here, too, data and analytics matter. Across several companies, I have observed that the social networks of women—whom they talk to, are friends with, and seek advice from—seem to be systematically smaller and less likely to extend up the hierarchy than men's networks.[12] That is a measure of inclusivity, or rather the lack of it. But even more important, the data can tell us how to correct this imbalance.

The instinct to send women off to a training workshop on 'how to network' may be the wrong one. In at least one case, we found that the difference between the scale and shape of men's and women's networks disappeared once we accounted for the position of the individual in the corporate hierarchy. Networks in this company tended to be larger and extended upwards the more senior you were, regardless of gender. Women just happened to be in more junior roles. The corrective action needed was to address imbalance in promotions, not necessarily giving women advice on how to schmooze better.

My point is that without data and analytics, discussions on diversity remain ideological, but with data, they become concrete and actionable management efforts. Digitalization provides that data and analytics capability.

A third major trend is **decentralization**—greater delegation and autonomy for an organization's members. If you've been following the current thinking in organization design, you've likely come across several prominent examples of organizations that are self-consciously decentralized. They include examples as diverse as Buurtzorg, a Dutch healthcare organization that operates as a vast collection of autonomous twelve-person units, and Valve, the Seattle-based gaming company known for its flat structure with only two layers separating the CEO from all other employees in a 500-person company. What is common to these is the extent to which they rely on digital technologies ranging from intranets to collaborative work management tools (that work similarly to Google Docs) to enable employees to manage themselves without the need for extensive managerial intervention.

Taking decentralization to an extreme level are a new breed of organizations known as decentralized autonomous organizations (DAOs), often built on blockchain technology. Many of these are in the cryptocurrency space. Whatever the eventual fate of cryptocurrencies, the idea of blockchain-based organizing, where groups operate as organizations using smart contracts and voting-based governance with no single hierarchical authority, is an interesting experiment.

While the economic significance of all these entities put together may not yet be substantial, they do hold a disproportionate mindshare in discussions about the future of work. I would wager that most top business school programmes worldwide teach about one or more of these organizations in their core Organizational Behaviour or Strategy classes. It seems clear that understanding their eventual viability cannot be separated from understanding the digital algorithms they rely on to organize themselves.

All these transformative trends—diversity initiatives, decentralization, distributed working—are riding on the fact that organizations are increasingly digital. For good or worse, digital algorithmic tools are part of the fabric of organizing today and their descendants will likely continue to be, in no small part because the value from aggregating this data and extracting intelligence from it is potentially so large. That brings us to artificial intelligence.

Why AI Is Central to Digitalization

Let's peel the onion a bit more. If digitalization is core to all other trends, AI is core to digitalization. If you think about the basic processes of digital transformation—representation, connectivity, aggregation—it should be apparent that aggregation is where a lot of the economic value really lies. Yet it can be a bottleneck. Digital representation produces data, and connectivity solves the logistical problem of getting digital data from one place to another and pooling it. These steps by themselves would still not be enough to extract anything useful from it.

In fact, the sheer volume of data being generated through digital representation and connectivity can make it harder, not easier, to do something with it, if the only thing we had to rely on were our human minds. The term 'bounded rationality' to describe how we think was coined by the polymath Herbert Alexander Simon. This incredible individual was a founder figure of not one but three modern scientific disciplines: computer science, cognitive science, and, my own field, organization science. (Incidentally, he also won a Nobel Prize in economics.)[13]

One of Simon's many lasting contributions was the idea that human beings are intendedly but only limitedly (hence 'boundedly') rational. He felt the need to make this argument in opposition to the prevailing orthodoxy in the economics of his time, which began with assumptions about human rationality that were unbounded—people were assumed to be capable of knowing pretty much everything and being able to process vast quantities of information without breaking a sweat.

Simon offered the much-needed corrective that such an assumption was not merely unrealistic (that by itself is rarely a problem in any science if it gets us to better prediction), but more importantly, the assumption was leading to bad theories and predictions that simply did not match what we observed. Subsequent work in psychology has given us a pretty good handle on the limits of human information processing as well as a deep understanding of the evolutionary history of our species that might have produced these limits. Today, the bounded rationality idea is a basic premise in organization science and has even taken root in parts of economics. The field of behavioural economics, for instance, would not exist without it.

All that said, the label 'bounded rationality' that Simon used is not one of my favourites. It seems a bit like saying 'non-yellow elephants'. The 'non-yellow' is redundant since that's the only kind of elephant there is. In much the same way, human rationality is what it is—unbounded rationality was, and still is, even in the age of AI, a theoretical fiction. But the fact remains that there are clear limits to the amount of information that humans can process, and given those limits, the data deluge created by digital representation and connectivity would very soon hit a wall in terms of what can usefully be done with it.

This is why aggregation, and in particular technology that allows us to perform this aggregation in a way that humans cannot, is so central to the digitalization story. Through connectivity of digitally represented content, we can pull it all together, but it is only when we aggregate it, extract insight and intelligence out of it, particularly using smart algorithms like artificial intelligence, that it all pays off. But when it does, it makes investments in digital representation and connectivity more valuable, which produce more data, which in turn make investments in aggregation more valuable, and so on. AI and the value it promises through the aggregation of data is what is likely to keep the digitalization loop spinning ever faster.

Artificial Intelligence: the Old and the New

At its core, AI refers to algorithms that can act (to a degree) intelligently. While it's been a philosophically thorny concept to define, computer scientists have converged on a definition of 'intelligence is as intelligence does'. A system, whether human or artificial, is considered intelligent if it can accomplish its goals across a wide range of circumstances. Intelligence is flexible goal pursuit.[14]

Algorithms are recipes. They involve a sequence of steps, including some possibly random elements, that result in an outcome. The steps could be written down in a language like English, as in instructions on how to open a bank account online, or symbols and pictograms, as in instructions on the emergency exit door in an aircraft. Sometimes they are not written down at all—as in the procedures by which teams of surgeons and nurses together conduct a complex operation, or a trio of Indian classical musicians (or a jazz quartet) manage to improvise together beautifully even if they have never met before. But make no mistake, there are rules at work, and acquiring them is an extensive part of the training in these professions.

Algorithms in this general sense have been with us for a long, long time, and cover everything from ancient cooking recipes found entombed with pharaohs to instructions for assembling IKEA furniture. But the ability to embed them in computer programs means they can draw on vast amounts of data as inputs, and even the most complex sequence of steps can be executed at lightning speed and millions of times without error. Artificial intelligence thus refers to digital algorithms written in the form of computer software that can act intelligently.

Even AI is not that new. The field of artificial intelligence has been around for more than seven decades and can be traced back to a very important conference held at Dartmouth in the 1950s (at which one of the important contributors was none other than

Herbert Simon). But what has changed in this millennium has been the kind of AI that we currently have. This is called machine learning, and in particular a variant of it called 'deep learning' has been revolutionary. An easy way to understand the difference between this newer machine learning-based AI and older AI, which is called rule-based AI, is to think of the following example:

Suppose you have to teach your ten-year-old child how to do long division. How would you do it? You write down the steps, walk them through it, and show them how to apply the steps. And hopefully they understand the rules and then they can apply it to do any long division problem they face. By giving them the rules (an algorithm!), you have enabled them to be intelligent in the domain of long division problems—they can solve a wide variety of them using the same rules.

Now contrast that with teaching the same ten-year-old how to ride a bicycle. We can't give them rules on how to ride a bicycle, at least not very useful ones ('don't fall off!'). They must figure it out for themselves. What you can give them is lots of experience in a safe context. You can show them through examples, and you can help them develop their own examples by trial and error from which they can learn their own rules. Those rules are tacit and buried deep in their minds and muscle memory, but they are rules about movement, force, weight, friction, and balance. What they're doing through trial and error (trial and terror, for some kids) is using their experience to infer the rules from the data. That's how machine learning works.

An analogy that might help you see it even more clearly is to think back to those problems that we used to have inflicted on us in school where they show you a series of shapes—a circle, a triangle, a star, a circle, a triangle—and then a question mark. What comes next (Figure 2)?

Figure 2: What comes next?

How do you solve this problem? You do it by inferring the pattern from the data. We've seen a few examples, and the pattern seems to be circle, triangle, star, then circle, triangle, star again, and so on. So, when you get circle, triangle, and a '?' you know what's coming next is a star. This is exactly how modern machine learning works, regardless of how sophisticated it is. The rule could be probabilistic—there will be a star with 70 per cent probability after a circle and a triangle, but that does not change the basic process. The sequence could be a large one, looking almost random to us boundedly rational humans, but if there is a pattern (e.g. after three triangles and two circles and one triangle you get a star), the machines can find it. There are, as you might imagine, many technical bells and whistles that I have skipped over, but the gist of it is, given enough data, if there's a pattern in the data, we now have machine learning algorithms that can find that pattern.[15]

All machine learning algorithms today, from the least sophisticated to the most cutting-edge technology, operate in a fundamental sense in the same way, and that is by learning rules (i.e. patterns) from data. These display intelligence (i.e. they pursue goals in a flexible manner) in two senses. First, these systems are flexible in the sense that the rules can be inferred from data with minimal human intervention rather than imposed by a human coder. Second, the inferred rules themselves are flexible in the sense they can account for a vast set of contingencies, unlike simple rules of the 'if X then Y' type. This is why machine learning is considered (somewhat) intelligent.

One terminological point to bear in mind here is that the final set of rules that have been learned is by itself an algorithm—a set of rules for predicting what's coming next. But there is also the algorithm for learning those rules from the data. These are rules about how to learn rules (a meta-algorithm if you like). AI as an algorithm for learning and the result of that learning process crystallized as an algorithm comprising a specific set of rules learned from data are two different uses of the term 'algorithm' in this context. This can sometimes lead to confusing conversations.

For instance, if the data is biased, the rules learned from the data will also be biased, resulting in a biased algorithm. But that does not imply that the meta-algorithm used to learn from the data is itself biased.

Prediction Is All You Need

Our little example with the circles, triangles, and stars should also help you see why modern AI based on machine learning has been dubbed a 'prediction machine'.[16] I like to think of it as an imperfect crystal ball. It predicts, but it doesn't get it right all the time for a variety of reasons. The most obvious one simply is the quality of the data we feed in it. The better the quality of data we give it, the clearer the pattern in the data—of course the crystal ball gets that much more powerful.

But at the core of it all, machine learning is driven by one underlying logic—given a lot of data, given a lot of processing power, if there is a pattern in the data, the algorithms can find it. And once it's found the pattern, it can use it to make predictions, exactly like in my triangle, circle, star problem. I can see what's coming next! And that ability to make predictions is enormously important.

Why? Because every decision we ever made in our lives, whether it's buying a car, buying a house, who to date, which job to do—each of these decisions relied on a prediction. You may not have thought about it explicitly like that, but that is very likely what is going on under the hood. Every decision between doing A and doing B relies intuitively on a prediction you're making in your mind about what will happen if I do A versus what will happen if I do B. Combining that prediction with some way of assessing how much you like the respective outcomes is what produces a decision. Now if you can use machine learning with a large amount of data and a lot of processing power to improve the quality of that prediction—what will happen when I do A versus what will happen when I do B—then of course your quality of decision-making will improve.

That's the core of why machine learning today is so important in a host of business applications, technical applications, and in shaping how organizations work. If there's a decision that needs to be made that can be anchored to an underlying prediction problem, and that prediction problem can be solved by using a lot of data in which there's a pattern that can be discovered, then even if our human minds can't discover that pattern, the algorithms can. In fact, even if no human expert could articulate the pattern they are relying on, the algorithms can discover it given enough data. Tacit knowledge is no defence against automation any more.

It is useful to distinguish here between stand-alone versus embedded decisions. A stand-alone decision looks like something you might imagine taking place in a boardroom with a bunch of people in business suits. Or you could imagine this just in your mind as you sit there pondering some important life choice— that's still a stand-alone decision. There's a clear choice you must make between a small set of alternatives, you get to pick one and that'll be it. But there are also embedded decisions that are really layers upon layers of micro decisions that aggregate up to produce an outcome.

An example is the way you navigate your way from one location in the city to another. You must make a series of decisions about where to turn left, which road to avoid, where the traffic might suggest you should take an alternative path, how fast you should drive, and so on. None of these feel like decisions as we are making them, but they're just happening subconsciously. A lot of the machine learning applications today have this flavour where they're making thousands, sometimes millions upon millions of tiny micro decisions that are embedded, but they all add up in the end to come up with a recommendation or a forecast or a particular output, such as 'watch this movie!' or 'hire this person' or 'go to the gym now!'

In fact, a lot of human behaviour is (implicit) decision-making. This was another of Herbert Simon's epiphanies. If we add that all decisions rely (at least implicitly) on predictions, and that AI algorithms can make such predictions based on patterns in data, it becomes easier to see why the ramifications of this technology are so enormous in all spheres of our lives.

Are developments in generative AI like large language models (LLMs) such as ChatGPT fundamentally different? They are not. Large language models also work in basically the same way as the triangle, circle, star example. Using a large amount of data, which in this case is the volume of text in various online libraries and the internet, the algorithms can find patterns in language. It turns out that the way we speak and write, while it may sound to us as if we are being very creative and novel each time we do it, is quite rule bound. There's a lot of pattern and structure in what we say and write, though our bounded rationality prevents us from seeing those patterns.

But the machines can, so that given enough data and given a few words as input (prompt), an LLM can reasonably predict what the next words are that should come, exactly like our triangle, circle, star problem. And given that prediction, it can go on to predict further from there, and keep going.

Generation of new content—text, images, sounds—can also be structured as a prediction problem. That's what large language models like GPT-4o and Claude 3 and image generation AI such as DALL-E and Stable Diffusion are doing. You put in some text, and the AI algorithm predicts what the next set of words (or pixels) that would be most appropriate given the text you fed. Some have pejoratively called these 'stochastic parrots'.[17] We don't need to discuss here whether we humans are also a species of stochastic parrot. Rather, the fact that we are finding LLMs so convincing and useful reinforces the point that parrots, even stochastic ones, have their uses.

Since LLMs essentially find linkages between sequences of data—words—one can also use the same basic technology to translate between languages, and GPT3.5 already did a pretty good job at this. But translation need not be between languages like Mandarin and Hindi alone. We could translate between English and Python code, or between the jargon of marketers and HR professionals, or between a sequence of genes and the proteins that are expressed by them. GPT stands for generative pre-trained transformer, but it is also a 'general-purpose translator', a sort of Babel fish that can work across conceptual domains.[18] And yet this all comes from brute force pattern detection in large volumes of data, not fundamentally different from our triangle, circle, and star problem.

To be sure, large language models have really been revolutionary because for the first time these predictions look and sound like humans. They talk to us like humans do, they draw images that we could imagine a human produced. They allow for 'conversational computing'—people without a background in computer science and programming can now interact with and instruct algorithms to solve the problem they need solved. LLMs answer questions, synthesize ideas, search, put together ideas from disparate domains, and integrate them. They can don synthetic personalities and role-play. They can come up with convincing critiques and contrarian viewpoints to help refine our own thinking.[19]

This is quite a remarkable breakthrough. My point, however, is that the underlying logic of how it works is still driven by the same basic machine learning methodology: given enough data and given powerful processing technologies, like deep learning architectures, if we can find patterns in the data, we can convert them into useful predictions. And those predictions in turn can then be used to make economically important decisions. Prediction is all you need.

Machine learning represents the victory of inductive, data-first approaches over deductive, theory-first approaches to solving a large variety of real-world problems, from playing games like chess to driving, and now to producing proofs in geometry, writing passable poetry, and creating beautiful images. We have discovered that many problems are better treated like learning how to bicycle and not like long division. Data—lots of it—not human-formulated rules, is what seems to work.

The bottleneck in the old rule-based approach, it turns out, was our own bounded rationality. To feed in rules we had to understand the patterns in a domain and then synthesize the rules in the language of math or code. Machine learning is certainly not unboundedly rational or omniscient—it is still restricted to only learning what it can from the data available to it, and much of human existence remains uncodified data. But it can detect and synthesize far more complex rules directly from the data, and it seems to be getting better at doing so without involving us or getting bottlenecked by our cognition. This is a higher degree of flexibility than older AI systems, and quite naturally, we consider these systems to be more intelligent.

That's powerful and exciting. But for human organizations, these digital technologies also pose a significant challenge.

The Co-Evolution of Algorithms and Organizations: A Timeline

There is an active debate in the computer science and AI community about the timeline over which AI will fully achieve human-like capacities across a broad range of domains—what is sometimes called artificial general intelligence or AGI. This would mean that we don't just have specialized algorithms that beat humans at chess or recognizing images but instead have a general-purpose intelligence that can effortlessly switch between and be effective in a wide range of problem domains.

Some observers refer to this event as the 'singularity'[20] and others worry about the extinction of humanity if we don't solve the problem of aligning this AI's interests with our own. But I do not know enough about computer science to offer a useful forecast about the timeline for the singularity and its consequences or even comment on the forecasts of others. That is why this is not a book about the singularity (or about killer AI robots either).

However, I do believe that the timeline for changes to organizations has two important points that will arrive almost certainly before the singularity ever does.

First, we do not need AGI to become a reality for us to reach a stage in which organizations can function without (m)any humans—what I call zero-human organizing. My reasoning is simple: under the logic of specialization, we have set up contemporary organizations in a way in which most of their members and employees, whether blue collar or white collar, don't really act like a general intelligence. An important consequence of the logic of specialization (that I will discuss in detail in Chapter 6) that pervades our economies is that it has narrowed the set of competencies among the individuals we recruit into organizations. That narrowing is precisely what makes human effort in organizations vulnerable to replacement by AI, which is still far short of general AI in terms of capabilities.

In an important sense, an organization is itself an algorithm. Ultimately, every organization is a system for turning certain inputs (employees, resources, tools) into outcomes (profits, social welfare) through a series of steps. Could an algorithm with human executors of the sequence be converted into one with digital sub-algorithms? Automation has demonstrated this is possible for some manual labour-intensive jobs with robotic factories and robotic farming and AGI can in principle do the same for knowledge work. Teams of AI agents working together to achieve goals was one of the big new ideas of 2024.[21]

I'm not offering a forecast on when this will be widely adopted, but I am stating that this can happen well before we attain something like artificial general intelligence. For long, economists and organization scientists converged on the view that while AI could take over low-skill tasks, those that required generating content and ideas were the prerogative of humans, so that AI technologies need not be net job destroyers.[22] I remain cautiously optimistic that this is still true, at least in the immediate future. The caution comes from the fact that many of us are beginning to doubt the permanence of this assumption after GPT3.5 launched in November 2022.

There is no law of nature that guarantees that when old jobs get replaced by technology, a net surplus of new jobs will inevitably be dreamed up by humans, for humans to perform. However often that happened in the past (and we know now it has not *always* happened), the past did not include anything like generative AI and large language models (LLMs). These technologies imply that machines on their own might be able to discover new opportunities, and also learn how to fulfil them without having to be given the rules for how to do so by humans.

Put differently, with further advances in AI, as with many technologies in the past, there may well be a flood of many new things to do, but they may not necessarily require humans to do them. Unless humans are needed to pursue those new opportunities, they have no economic power, and without the demand they generate, the virtuous cycle of technology displacing some jobs but creating many more can grind to a halt. This may not happen tomorrow, but there is no reason to believe it can *never* happen.

The rapid pace of developments in generative AI and LLMs have white-collar workers from managers to research scientists beginning to ask themselves if they will experience what blue-collar workers did with automation. There are things I can do today with these technologies in a matter of minutes, things that would have taken a research assistant many hours, if not days. I happen to think that this is a very bad reason to stop using human research assistants (as I will elaborate on in Chapter 5), but I doubt I will be in the majority if the productivity of the AI tools keeps improving.

For individual organizations competing against each other, the race to improve productivity may leave little room to consider alternative technological trajectories that focus on keeping humans employable. The implications of (near) zero-human organizing for jobs, social security, and political stability will be enormous, and we will need some very creative thinking from economists and policymakers (and some robust wealth redistribution) to prepare for this eventuality even if it never fully materializes. I believe it is policymakers and governments who play the primary role in shaping the speed and trajectory of our journey towards zero-human organizations, not the designers and members of typical organizations, so this is not a book about the risk of AI-driven unemployment either.

This does not at all mean that I am unconcerned about the impact of digital technologies on employment! I have not focused on this question simply because I do not have much to add over what others have already said. Economists John Autor and Daron Acemoglu have conducted some of the most careful thinking about this question, and to me, they do not sound very sanguine about the long-term prospects for human employment because of AI.[23] One of Autor's recent papers has a title that says it all: 'The Labor Market Impacts of Technological Change: From Unbridled Enthusiasm to Qualified Optimism to Vast Uncertainty.' David Susskind has documented, quite brilliantly, the dramatic change in thinking among economists about the effects of technology on employment.[24]

Rather, my focus is on what will happen to the humans (still) inside organizations—and also why that is likely to be a relevant concern for a meaningful period.[25] I don't think we know enough yet to be able to forecast when (and if) zero-human organizing will become widespread. What we do know with a high degree of confidence is that well before the advent of zero-human organizing, we are likely to see widespread bionic organizing, which I define as an integration of digital algorithms into organizations (Figure 3).

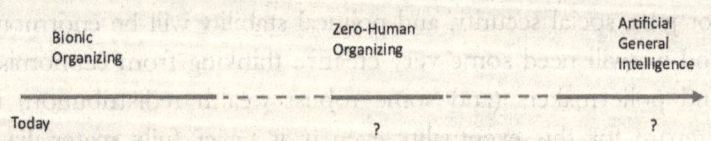

Figure 3: A possible timeline

The term 'bionic' was originally coined to refer to electronic systems inspired by biology.[26] I'll borrow it to serve as a useful shorthand for indicating an organization that has become deeply infused with digital algorithmic technologies, including AI.

This integration is well underway, and takes two distinct forms, though the extent of integration across these forms is uneven today.

The first form of integration is the adoption of digital algorithms as *tools* in organizations. This has happened so rapidly that we may not even have paid it much attention. Nearly everything we do in organizations such as hiring, planning, and execution has become heavily reliant on various forms of software (i.e. digital algorithms) from email, ERP systems, databases, Zoom and cloud-based collaboration technologies all the way to AI and robotics. In this sense, most organizations today are already bionic.

Here is a simple thought experiment: Imagine your organization gets hit by an electromagnetic pulse that knocks out every electronic system for an indefinite period of time. Would you still be functional, even for a day? If the answer is no, then you are in a bionic organization. Given the positive feedback cycle between digital representation, connection, and aggregation, there seems to be little doubt that many if not all these tools will embed AI of some sort. It was already in your email programs, predicting what emails are spam, for a long time, and now we have the AI assistant that can summarize in real time the takeaways and action items of the Zoom meeting that you zombied your way through.

A second form of integration involves digital algorithms, particularly AI, as 'teammates'. I put in the scare quotes here to make clear that I am not implying a moral equivalence between working with people and working with machines. But I am implying a form of working together that goes beyond the use of algorithms by humans to help make decisions—rather we are talking about intelligent agents that have some degree of decision rights.

My collaborator Bart Vanneste and I analysed the idea that AI systems today display various degrees of 'agency'—the capacity to think, plan, and act. The extent of agency that we perceive in AI systems has significant consequences for how much we trust them as teammates. It may also shape how much agency we believe we have when dealing with them.[27]

You might argue that as long as a human makes final decisions, the AI only remains a tool. But by this reasoning most human workers in organizations are also acting as tools to the extent that their decisions require final approval by hierarchical superiors.

Conversely, we could argue that the use of AI as a teammate is nothing but the use of AI as a tool with some degree of delegation. The reality is that in large volume transactions such as insurance claims processing, invoice approval, trading recommendations, and CV screening, AI use is already prevalent in which the machine makes a decision without further approval or review by human managers.[28] To the extent that the adoption of digital algorithms and AI improves productivity (and it seems clear that they often do), it is difficult to imagine goal-centric organizations resisting their adoption, and this is the reason we are well on our way down the path to cementing a bionic future for organizations.

The Future of Organizations is Bionic for Now

Engineers talk about the 'design period' of a project. This is the time over which the formulated design for a project must be effective. The design period for the ideas in this book is not measured in months or years but lasts as long as we continue to have bionic organizations (or conversely, till we get to zero-human organizing). But given the rapid pace of developments in AI, you might well ask, why is it reasonable to assume the bionic age of organizations will last long enough to be even worth planning for? In the longer term, will humans have any advantages left (over AI) that will make it necessary for organizations to still include them?

To answer these questions, I need to ask you one of my own. **Do you think the human mind does anything more**

than information processing? In other words, do you believe
that what our brains do is more than just extremely sophisticated
manipulation of data and information? If you answer 'Yes', you
probably see the difference between AI and humans as a chasm—
one which can never be bridged, and which implies our design
period is quite long.

As it happens, my own answer to my question is 'No'. In the
longer term, I simply don't feel confident that we can rule out
technologies that can replicate and surpass everything humans
currently do. If it's all information processing, there is no reason to
believe that it is physically impossible to create better information
processing systems than what natural selection has made out of
us. However, I do believe our design period for bionic organizing
is still at least decades long, if not more. This is because time is on
the side of homo sapiens. I mean both individual lifetimes, as well
as the evolutionary time that has brought our species to where it is.

Over our individual lifetimes, the volume of data each one
of us is exposed to in the form of sound, sight, taste, touch,
and smell—and only much later, text—is so large that even the
largest large language model looks like a toy in comparison. As
computer scientist Yann LeCun, who led AI at Meta, recently
observed, human babies absorb about fifty times more visual
data alone by the time they are four years old than the text data
that went into training an LLM like GPT3.5.[29] A human would
take multiple lifetimes to read all that text data, so that is clearly
not where our intelligence (primarily) comes from. Further, it is
also likely that the sequence in which one receives and processes
this enormous quantity of data matters, not just being able to
receive a single one-time data dump, even if that were possible
(currently it is not).

This comparison of data access advantages that humans
have over machines implicitly assumes the quality of processing
architecture is comparable between humans and machines.

But even that is not true. In evolutionary time, we have existed as a distinct species for at least 200,000 years. I estimate that gives us more than 100 billion distinct individuals. Every child born into this world comes with slightly different neuronal wiring and over the course of its life will acquire very different data. Natural selection operates on these variations and selects for fitness. This is what human engineers are competing against when they conduct experiments on different model architectures to find the kind of improvements that natural selection has found through blind variation, selection, and retention. Ingenious as engineers are, at this point, natural selection has a large 'head' start (if you will pardon the pun).

This is manifested in the far wider set of functionalities that our minds display compared to even the most cutting-edge AI today (we are after all the original—and natural—general intelligences!). We not only remember and reason, we also do so in ways that involve affect, empathy, abstraction, logic, and analogy. These capabilities are all, at best, nascent in AI technologies today. It's not surprising that these are the very capabilities in humans that are forecast to be in high demand soon.[30]

Our advantage is also manifest in the energy efficiency of our brains. By the age of twenty-five, I estimate that our brain consumes about 2,500 kWh; GPT3 is believed to have used about 1 million kWh for training. AI engineers have a long way to go to optimize energy consumption in training and deployment of their models before they can begin to approach human efficiency levels. Even if machines surpass human capabilities through extraordinary increases in data and processing power (and the magic of quantum computing, as some enthusiasts argue), it may not be economical to deploy them for a long time yet. In Chapter 5, I will give more reasons why humans can be useful in bionic organizations, even if they underperform algorithms, as long as they are different from algorithms in what they know. That diversity seems secure because of the unique data we possess, as I argued above.

Note that I have not felt the need to invoke the most important reason I can think of for continued human involvement in organizations: we might just like it that way since we are a group-living species. Researchers studying guaranteed basic income schemes are finding that people want to belong to and work in organizations even if they do not need the money.[31] Rather, I am saying that purely goal-centric reasons alone are sufficient for us to expect a bionic (near) future.

That said, none of this is a case for complacency about either employment opportunities for humans (a problem for policymakers), or the working conditions of humans in organizations (which is what I focus on). We do not need AI technologies to match or exceed human capabilities for them to play a significant role in our organizational life, for worse and for better. We already live in bionic organizations and the way we develop them further can either create a larger and widening gap between goal and human centricity or help bridge that gap. Technologies for monitoring, control, hyper-specialization, and the atomization of work do not need to be as intelligent as us to make our lives miserable. Only their deployers—other humans—do.

We are already beginning to see serious questions raised about the organizational contexts that digital technologies create in bionic organizations. For instance, what does it mean for our performance to be constantly measured and even predicted? For our behaviour to be directed, shaped, and nudged by algorithms, with or without our awareness? What does it mean to work alongside an AI that is basically opaque to you about its inner workings? That can see complex patterns in data that you cannot? That can learn from you far more rapidly than you can learn from it? That is controlled by your employer in a way that no co-worker can be?

Conclusion

The digitalization of organizations is gathering momentum, through the mutually reinforcing processes of representation, connection, and aggregation. Advances in AI technologies promise to unlock enormous value from aggregation and are therefore likely to hasten digitalization.

In this chapter, I have explained how modern AI works, and why it is different from other digital technologies in terms of the implications for human organizations. Organizations in the near future will almost certainly feature a mix of human and algorithmic intelligences—they will be 'bionic'. They may well have fewer humans per organization than they currently do, and those humans might be doing jobs that do not exist today, with a different set of skills, but bionic organizations will contain humans.

This raises challenges at three distinct levels: for policymakers (involving economic growth, employment, and equity), for leaders of organizations (concerning organizational change, the management of human capital, and employee welfare), and for individuals (seeking to build meaningful and viable careers in an ecology of bionic organizations). I focus on the second and the third set of issues in this book.

The core question I am concerned with is this: Can bionic organizations meet the twin objectives of being both goal-centric and human-centric? Or will the changes being brought about by digital algorithms make organizations fundamentally inhospitable for the people left in them, the only respite perhaps being zero-human organizing, when (and if) that arrives? Should we care and if yes, what can we do about it?

Answering these questions, or at least offering a framework to think about them, is what I focus on for the rest of this book.

Chapter 3

What Remains Constant

You're staring at two envelopes, one blue, one red, hardly able to believe your eyes. After multiple rounds of interviews and weeks of intensive preparation and negotiation, you now have what you wanted all along—job offers for the same rank and job description from the two top employers in your industry.

The red envelope is from Alpha Corp. As you look over notes from your research on the company, you recall being struck by how professional and structured the work environment in the company had seemed. There was little doubt as to who was in charge and the culture placed a premium on successful execution of corporate mandates. Alpha Corp took a no- nonsense approach to how it treated its employees—they paid well and expected good performance. They did not believe in 'wasting the time' of their employees on training programmes and corporate retreats. Relationships between people appeared cordial and professional, though it seemed unlikely that colleagues would ever see each other between Friday evening and Monday morning. Everyone understood this was a meritocracy, some people made more money and had the corner offices, but that was life. Alpha had a very successful business model and took pains to make sure to continue smoothly executing this model. 'If you want to try something new,' you recall being told with a smile by the HR manager in one of the interviews, 'take a cooking class on the weekends!' The salary offer from Alpha was well above industry average.

As you open the blue envelope containing Omega Corp's offer, you notice that the stationery seems customized to the manager who has sent you the offer. Omega operated a high delegation system, and employees had considerable leeway in how they met their objectives. You were expected to do things your own way, 'as long as you become an expert at doing it!' one of the recruiters had said. Omega Corp took employee training seriously. The offer letter described a plethora of learning opportunities and mentorship programmes that allowed employees to enhance their skills. There was the possibility of setting aside some time to work on new ideas and projects, too, if they supported Omega's mission to become a socially responsible organization. The letter welcomes you to become a part of the Omega 'team', and the word does not seem misplaced. You recall that many of the colleagues you met seemed to know each other very well and they probably hung out after work, too, with families. Your recollection from your interviews is of a collegial place and the second page of your offer letter has been signed by all the members of the team you would potentially be joining. The letter goes on to explain at some length why your salary offer was a fair one, and shows the distribution of pay at the rank you are being recruited for.

The salary offer from Omega is also well above industry average, but is 5 per cent below that of Alpha Corp.

Which offer will you take?

Regardless of where in the world you are, or what cultural and demographic background you come from come, I believe the chances are quite high that you will take the offer from Omega rather than that from Alpha. That's what most of the participants from most of my classes where I have run this little experiment do. The blue envelope almost always trumps the red one (with apologies to Morpheus).

You might think MBA students and executives in my classes at INSEAD—diverse though they are—are hardly a representative sample, and you'd be right. That's why I also ran a similar exercise with 500 respondents from an online survey platform. The respondents were 53 per cent female, 33 per cent non-white, with an average age of thirty-four (range nineteen to eighty) and came from more than thirty countries. And yet an overwhelming majority (74 per cent) chose Omega (the blue envelope).

Why? Because at a basic level, people have preferences for the kinds of organizational contexts they want to work in. Omega Corp is organized in a way that is likely to satisfy those preferences for many people, but Alpha Corp is not.

We do not have to rely only on my data, illustrative though they are; after all, people who take online surveys are not representative of all humanity. Rather, an extensive review of prior research leads me to argue that the basic structure of these preferences for organizational contexts is unlikely to change anytime soon, digitalization notwithstanding. Furthermore, if we understand the structure of these preferences, we would have grasped the secret of what makes an organization human-centric.

Organizational Context Preferences

The design and context of an organization are related but not the same. An organization's design is manifested in its structure, patterns of interaction, and hiring and retention processes, which ideally come together to support the organization's goals (I'll say a lot more about design in Chapters 4–7). In contrast, the context refers to what the members of an organization observe and experience when they live in that organizational design. For instance, an organization might rely heavily on a design that emphasizes specialization and active monitoring and supervision by managers. The resulting organizational context may be experienced by employees as low in autonomy but with competent and supportive management. It's unlikely that an organization's members will have strong preferences directly for kinds of designs per se, but much more likely that they have preferences for the kinds of organizational contexts those designs generate.

I intentionally take an expansive view of what 'context' covers here. It includes culture, managerial practices, and the organization's mission, which are often and justifiably treated as distinct. However, my goal is to focus on what members of an organization perceive in aggregate about the experience of belonging to the organization they inhabit—the 'employee experience' if you like. I will (shortly) be far more precise in describing the dimensions along which organizational contexts vary.

Let's define an individual's organizational context preferences (OCPs) as **the ranking they assign to different organizational contexts based on their desirability, holding monetary compensation, and its equivalents constant.**[32] If people did not have OCPs, then given the same pay and material benefits (such as opportunities for promotions and raises, healthcare and benefits, pensions), they would be indifferent to other aspects of what life in the organization felt like. The fact that most people prefer Omega Corp over Alpha Corp despite the pay being 5 per cent lower tells us that this is highly unlikely.

In fact, it also tells us that not only do people have OCPs, they may also be willing, at least to some extent, to trade-off pay in order to satisfy these preferences. I have not explored how much of a pay cut people would be willing to take to join Omega over Alpha, but I'm confident that for at least some people, the number will be significantly higher than 5 per cent. The overwhelming evidence from systematic studies others have conducted is quite clear on both points: people value things besides money (and its equivalents) from their organizational contexts, and they are willing to trade-off between the two.[33]

Why does this matter?

First, catering to OCPs is a form of reward. When attempting to attract and retain members, it is important to bear in mind that the 'total compensation' an organization is offering consists not only of material rewards, but also the extent to which OCPs are being satisfied, or not.[34]

Second, satisfying OCPs is not merely motivating, but it may produce a particular kind of motivation—intrinsic motivation. This means that members would contribute effort towards the organization's objectives even if they were not being monitored. Specifying what we want from employees is notoriously hard and, in many circumstances, no formal rules can hope to capture the spirit of what we want perfectly.[35] To the extent that work is difficult to specify, measure, and monitor, you have to count on intrinsic motivation.

Third, in general people will differ in their OCPs and through careful selection and sorting in addition to design, organizations can match the kind of individuals they recruit to the context that their design creates. If the match is good, the result can be an extra bump in intrinsic motivation, which can lower the salary and supervision costs for employers as well as increase engagement with and enjoyment of the organizational context for employees.

The share prices of companies whose employees seem engaged and satisfied with their organizational contexts are known to reliably go up.[36] The implication is that even if you can pay the highest salaries in the industry, if the nature of work makes it difficult to monitor and measure, then matching on and satisfying OCPs becomes important.[37] And of course, by definition, since most employers cannot pay the highest salaries, satisfying OCPs is another possible path to competing for talent. Just as product differentiation helps compete for customers, differentiation on organizational context can help compete for employees.

It's also important to acknowledge that for a significant minority of people, little else appears to matter beyond material rewards from the organizational contexts they work in. When I analysed the open-ended text responses to extract the key reasons for why respondents chose Omega over Alpha so overwhelmingly, the themes indicate OCPs related to collegial work environment, training opportunities, company culture, and salary. But equally interesting are the reasons the 25 per cent who opt for Alpha (and the 5 per cent more money) typically provide: it's not that they care nothing about factors like collegial environments, training, and culture, they just prefer to get those things outside the work context. This is what other studies have also found.[38]

Let me summarize the three reasons I have given so far, for why OCPs matter. Since catering to OCPs is a form of reward that produces intrinsic motivation, and people differ in their OCPs, even the most goal-centric designs of organizations must consider the OCPs of the members it wants to recruit and retain if the nature of work makes it hard to monitor and requires intrinsic motivation, and if they want to attract talent without breaking the salary budget.

But beyond acting as a basis to build effective goal-centric designs, I believe OCPs also matter for a fourth reason: they give us a basis for defining what makes an organization human-centric.

Measuring Human Centricity in Organizations

If organizations are designed by humans for humans to operate in, aren't their designs, by definition, human-centric? Not necessarily. Consider the definition of 'human-centred design' used by the International Standards Organization (ISO):

'Human-centered design is an approach to interactive systems development that aims to make systems usable and useful by focusing on the users, their needs and requirements, and by applying human factors/ergonomics, and usability knowledge and techniques. This approach enhances effectiveness and efficiency, improves human well-being, user satisfaction, accessibility, and sustainability; and counteracts possible adverse effects of use on human health, safety, and performance.'

—ISO 9241-210:2019(E)

This perspective puts humans in the role of being served by the system being designed. Organizations, when they are purely goal-centric do the opposite: it's members are inputs, not users (in the sense the organization was not designed with their members' utility as the objective; at best it may have been a constraint). To be human-centric in the sense noted above, an organization would have to be designed with the preferences of its human members in mind and not only their human designer's preferences, which usually align with making the organization as goal-centric as possible.

Designing for the objective of meeting the company owner's goals (for instance, to become as wealthy as possible, under the logic of shareholder value maximization) does not make the company human-centric; meeting the OCPs of its employees does. Firms pursuing the goal of maximizing profits may or may not automatically be human-centric organizations, and vice versa. However, as we have seen, there are good reasons why the company's owners should be concerned with the OCPs of the employees even if ultimately the objective is to make the organization as goal-centric as possible (and the goal may well be profit maximization), because that's how they can provide intrinsic motivation and compete for talent without breaking the budget. Conversely, even the most human-centric founder must make sure their organization is economically viable.

When thinking about the broader challenge posed by digital technologies to the human centricity of organizations, we must be able to say something about OCPs that should apply to most (if not all) humans. But here's the catch: the members of any given organization with their unique OCPs represent *some* humans. How can we go from these individuals to statements about human centricity in general? If people's OCPs are different, does this imply that every organization will be human centric in a different way? Are we limited to saying, 'just make sure you don't undermine the things your organizations' members seem to value besides pay'? In other words, how can we say anything universal about what it takes for an organization to be human-centric, let alone how to retain human centricity in the face of rapid digitalization?

Can we dare describe a 'total utility' function for humans that is universal?

This is not a new problem. Seventy-five years ago, after the horrors of World War II, the United Nations oversaw the drafting and announcement of the Universal Declaration of Human Rights (UDHR). It was controversial when adopted (eight countries abstained from voting) and remains so to some extent today. Yet its impact is not in doubt—though it has no legally binding status, it has influenced law in many countries, and is seen as the cornerstone of the international human rights regime today.

I also want to highlight here its intellectual ambition, which was to define what humans universally value, regardless of their ethnicity, culture, or gender. The UDHR is written as a set of rights (e.g., the right to freedom of expression), but one can reverse engineer the assumptions about universal human values the authors made when they argued that these rights were worth having (try it yourself).[39] The list that emerges is reassuringly familiar: it includes autonomy, expectations of fair treatment, social affiliation, and belonging (besides health, safety, and economic well-being).

I believe we can do even better now. In the several decades since the UDHR was written, research in anthropology and social and evolutionary psychology has given us many insights about what people might universally want from the social contexts they inhabit. Further, this research shows us how there can be huge variation across people in their OCPs, even though the dimensions along which these preferences are defined are universal.

Sounds paradoxical? It isn't, really. Here's an analogy.[40] Every human tongue has receptor taste buds that respond to five basic kinds of tastes—sweet, sour, salty, bitter, and umami. But people differ enormously in their actual preferences—some prefer their snacks salty and some prefer them sweet. So, while the dimensions of taste are universal, the actual tastes vary a lot between any two individuals because of the weights they place on these dimensions. Differences in weights can arise from differences in the cultures one belongs to as well as individual differences.

An extensive body of research suggests that there is in fact a small, and universal, set of stable dimensions along which OCPs can be defined. The most likely reason these psychological needs are universal is that human psychology, as it pertains to living and operating in a group, has biological roots. That biology itself is the result of evolution, and all humans share a common evolutionary history in which living in groups and competing effectively against other groups was crucial, just as competition within groups was inescapable.

'Selfishness beats altruism within groups. Altruistic groups beat selfish groups. Everything else is commentary.'[41] That's the catchy summary offered by the two biologists David S. Wilson and E.O. Wilson, who are the architects of this theoretical synthesis. This evolutionary process has led to an interlocking set of biologically hardwired preferences and behaviours in group contexts that strike a delicate balance between promoting individual interests within groups while allowing groups to act cohesively in competition with other groups.

The process of biological evolution is slow and has taken tens of thousands of years to produce differences we can easily perceive. On the other hand, cultures (i.e. shared systems of beliefs and values) diverged as humans spread across this planet, and culture continues to evolve rapidly (and this may even be speeding up). That is why we might be culturally extremely differentiated and becoming more so, but since biological evolution operates far more slowly, it leaves its common traces in all of us. Further, these traces are likely to remain for significant portions of the future for the same reason—biological evolution is just very slow compared to cultural evolution. The result is a degree of universality and stability at the level of the dimensions that matter in the organizational contexts we prefer to inhabit.

I can't stress enough that **universal dimensions of OCPs do not imply that people's OCPs are universal.** There are multiple layers of differences across people in their OCPs. There are differences across cultures at the national, regional, community, and organizational levels, differences within cultures between people, and differences within a person over time. The universality lies in the dimensions we use to understand these differences, and the differences can be thought of as arising from the 'tuning' created by the cultures and circumstances we find ourselves in. But the OCP dimensions do impose universal limits on what people would find unacceptable—such as situations where none of these preferences were satisfied. The number of ways in which we can organize homo sapiens in a manner that satisfies them is not infinite.

So, what are these dimensions for describing how people derive intrinsic motivation from their organizational contexts? I draw heavily on the work of Edward Deci and Richard Ryan,[42] supplemented by my own review of the related literature. There are three primary dimensions that come directly from Deci and Ryan's work, and three secondary dimensions that appear to be derivative of the primary ones. **The roots of these dimensions can be traced to our evolutionary history as a**

group-living species. The evidence I came across in my review really leaves little room for doubt that these dimensions matter and must be accounted for in the 'total compensation package' an organization provides, and organization designers can only ignore these at their peril. My back pocket (or rather the endnotes) is bulging with references and notes for the interested reader who would like to verify this claim.[43]

1. **Autonomy**

    Organizational contexts vary in the extent to which they provide autonomy to individuals—the sense that they can choose and act freely without being unduly influenced or coerced by others. The opposite of a sense of autonomy is a sense of being controlled. Our aversion to being controlled is so strong that in some situations, people would rather forego benefits or incur harms than allow themselves to be controlled by even benign others.[44] (Anybody who has raised teenagers will know what I am talking about.) The preference for autonomy in organizational contexts is believed to originate in our evolutionary heritage to protect our individual interests, even though we are a group-living species, because of the balance that natural selection has had to strike between the individual and the group.

    The evidence strongly indicates that autonomy in terms of selecting and executing one's tasks or participation in decisions that affect oneself is highly motivating, and people make career choices trading off salary for autonomy in various forms (such as flexible hours, work-life balance, and the freedom to work from home, for instance). This suggests that management styles that emphasize delegation (i.e. holding subordinates accountable for outcomes) rather than direction (i.e.

enforce compliance to standards of behaviour) are intrinsically more motivating, all else being equal. The caveat that all other things must be held constant is important, because being held accountable for outcomes can increase the burden of risk when outcomes are variable. Therefore, an increase in autonomy is not automatically a good thing from an individual's perspective but must be traded-off against the additional risk bearing.

Of course, providing autonomy does not come for free; a manager who is ultimately accountable may risk ceding control and possible breakdowns of coordination among subordinates by over-delegating to them. Further, the desire for one's own autonomy does not rule out the desire to dominate others, which some people seem to have far more of than others. Providing more autonomy must be accompanied by safeguards against the rise to dominance of those so inclined, and a preference for autonomy should not be assumed to equal a preference for egalitarianism.

2. Relatedness

Organizational contexts vary in the extent to which they produce perceptions of relatedness in terms of feeling connected to others, forming meaningful relationships with them and a sense of belonging. Feeling connected to and identifying with a group is satisfying, and also useful for the group to accomplish collective goals through collaboration. Strong cultures, in which members share a few core beliefs and values, can produce a strong sense of relatedness. The preference for contexts that feature relatedness is likely to be an evolutionary adaptation in response to inter-group competition. Relatedness directly aligns individual efforts to group goals because it allows for them to subsume their own interests in favour of what is useful for the group.

There can also be costs to fostering relatedness. Necessary design and management decisions that adversely affect a few may have ripple-out consequences for the many in organizational contexts that are high on relatedness. For instance, suppose business conditions change and some parts of a business have to be divested. In organizational contexts that embody a strong sense of relatedness, the negative effects on motivation for those employees who stay on might be large.

3. Competence

Organizational contexts vary in the extent to which they support an individual's desire to feel competent—their sense of being and becoming more capable, in control of and effective at what they do. This implies opportunities for learning, training, and skill enhancement, as well as task allocations that stretch but do not exceed capabilities.

Though my focus has been on the dimensions of OCPs related to intrinsic motivation, meeting competence needs can also produce extrinsic motivation. In addition to satisfaction from a 'job well done', there can also be benefits in the form of acclaim and prestige (besides any monetary rewards the organization may bestow for competent performance). Recognition and appreciation are valuable by-products of competence for both the individual and the organization, because the satisfaction one derives from exhibiting competence can align individual to group goals, as prestige and acclaim flow from doing what is useful for the group.

The cost of building a context that meets people's needs for feeling competent is time and tolerance for failure because it takes experience and learning to develop competence.

The next three are not part of Deci and Ryan's framework but are also well represented in the literature. They appear to build on combinations of the primary dimensions, and there may be considerable variation in how they are met (and interpreted) across contexts.

4. Fairness

Organizational contexts vary in whether they are perceived as featuring fair treatment of their members (the meaning of fairness may vary across situations—fairness can mean equitable, not necessarily equal or vice versa). This pertains to pay as well as other benefits. Fairness is closely associated with connectedness, as being treated fairly enhances the sense of belonging to the organization. Fairness may also be a recognition of autonomy and individuality. Transparency in decisions affecting an organization's members, and due process in reaching those decisions, both contribute to an organizational context that is viewed as fair.

The costs incurred to be fair include the need for detailed explanation and documentation, as well as the harmful consequences of envy when differences in outcomes become widely visible.

5. Collective purpose

Organizational contexts vary in the extent to which they are characterized by a goal to accomplish something that has implications beyond the individual—for the organization or even the broader society at large. This is also referred to as a sense of 'mission'. Both competence and relatedness are linked to this dimension as purpose involves competence towards a collective goal. The specific mission of course varies widely across organizations. Purpose may motivate in immediate forms such as specific events and rituals, but over longer time periods as a shared understanding of what the collective is pursuing.

Getting alignment on common purpose requires significant efforts at socialization and selection of an organization's members. It can also mean restricting the pool from which one hires, and possibly losing some aspects of diversity in thinking.

6. Novelty

Finally, organizational contexts vary in the extent they cater to an individual's need for doing something novel—feed their curiosity. The pursuit of novelty is linked to autonomy and competence as it requires the freedom to explore as well as the sense of successful exploration that comes from having one's curiosity satisfied. What counts as novel will vary by situation.

One way to conduct a sanity check on this list is to ask what employees like (and dislike) about the organizational contexts their employers provide. So that's what my collaborator Nghi Truong and I (indirectly) did, with about 5.5 million employees in nearly 400,000 companies operating in 142 industrial segments in the US. The data comes from the employee review website Glassdoor for the years 2019 and 2020. It is humanly impossible to read these reviews and classify them at this scale, so the data was analysed using AI algorithms for extracting the salient topics from this mass of text.

We then classified the resulting set of topics along the six dimensions of OCPs. Finally, we counted fractions of the reviews that mentioned each dimension when describing what the writers liked about their organizations.

We can assume that the dimensions appearing here are both important to the reviewers and are being satisfied by their organizational contexts, while acknowledging that there could be dimensions that are important but not provided by the organization's context (more on this below).

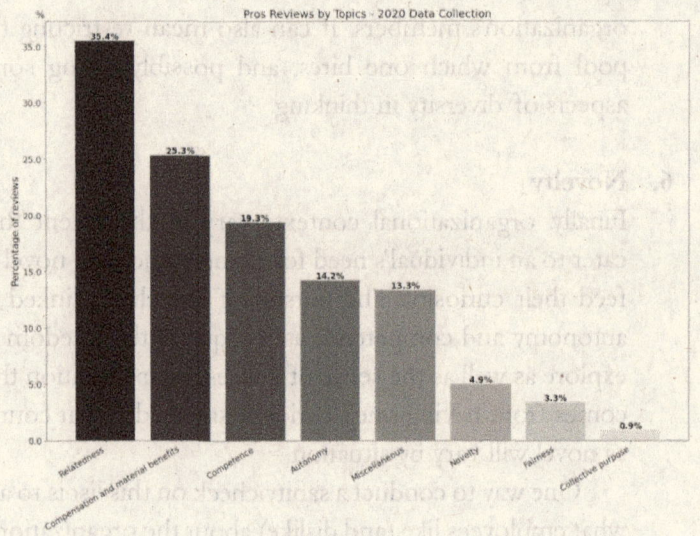

Figure 4a: What employees say they like about
their organizations

The number one attribute that employees like about their organizations is the sense of relatedness they experience with their co-workers. Nearly 35 per cent of the reviews in our data mentioned this as a positive aspect of their organization's context, and they used words like 'friendly', 'relaxing and fun', 'supportive', 'caring', 'family oriented', and 'family like' to describe it. Compensation and benefits came in second at 25 per cent. Competence (19 per cent) and Autonomy (14 per cent) came in next, with at least one of the attributes of Fairness, Novelty, and Purpose featuring in about 9 per cent of the reviews.

An advantage of the Glassdoor data is that employees state both the pros and cons of their organizational context, so we can also see what they dislike about their organizations. Here is what they see as cons of their organizational context.

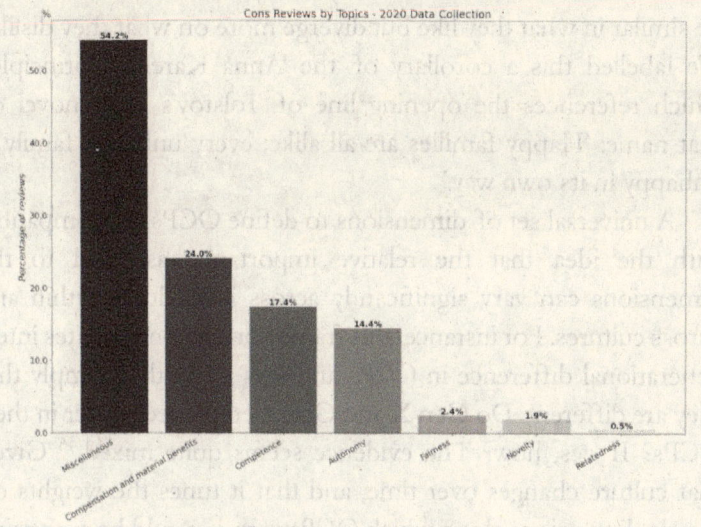

Figure 4b: What employees say they dislike
about their organizations

Interpreting these is a bit harder, because what does not appear here could be unimportant to the reviewer, or important but well satisfied by the organization.

What does appear is an important but unmet preference. The thing that people complain (coherently) the most about is compensation (24 per cent of reviews), followed closely by insufficient opportunities for developing competence (19 per cent) and experiencing autonomy (14 per cent). The first bar (54 per cent) is called miscellaneous because it was hard to decipher a single coherent topic (though many themes were broadly about negative aspects of the organizational culture). People, it seems, vary widely in what they complain about but are much more convergent in what they like.

My co-author Arianna Marchetti and I had discovered something similar when working with a different slice of the Glassdoor data (which ended in 2018).[45] By analysing each company's reviews separately (thank goodness for AI algorithms!), we found that reviewers were likely over time and in older firms to be similar in what they like but diverge more on what they dislike. We labelled this a corollary of the 'Anna Karenina principle', which references the opening line of Tolstoy's great novel of that name: 'Happy families are all alike; every unhappy family is unhappy in its own way.'

A universal set of dimensions to define OCPs are compatible with the idea that the relative importance assigned to the dimensions can vary significantly across individuals within and across cultures. For instance, this framework accommodates inter-generational difference in OCPs and says more than simply that they are different. Do Gen X and Gen Z employees differ in their OCPs? If yes, how? The evidence seems quite mixed.[46] Given that culture changes over time, and that it tunes the weights on the six dimensions along which OCPs vary, it would be surprising if there were no intergenerational differences in what employees want from their organizational contexts.

But we could also say that one systematic source of difference in OCPs that should arise across generations (and indeed countries) is in how they trade-off material compensation for OCPs. OCPs should matter more during periods of economic prosperity and less during recessions; and should matter more in prosperous countries than in economically weaker countries.

The World Values Survey gives us some insight into how one of the core dimensions of OCP—autonomy—is differentially important across generations.[47] Nghi Truong also helped me analyse data from about 450,000 respondents collected over seven waves across 109 countries between 1982 and 2022. Surprisingly, the evidence is that over time, autonomy has become more important for all age groups—it is not the case that Gen Z consider autonomy more important than Gen X.

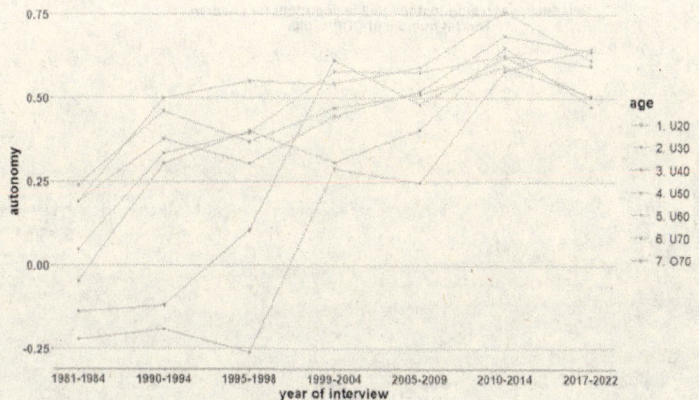

Figure 5: Autonomy preferences across waves of the
World Values Survey

Rather, a bigger difference is by economic prosperity. Data from
the same source also tells us that in the top quartile of GDP per
capita countries, parents are more likely to raise their children to be
independent and place less emphasis on obedience (these children
will presumably grow into adults who seek more autonomy) than
parents in the countries that are in the bottom quartile of GDP
per capita.

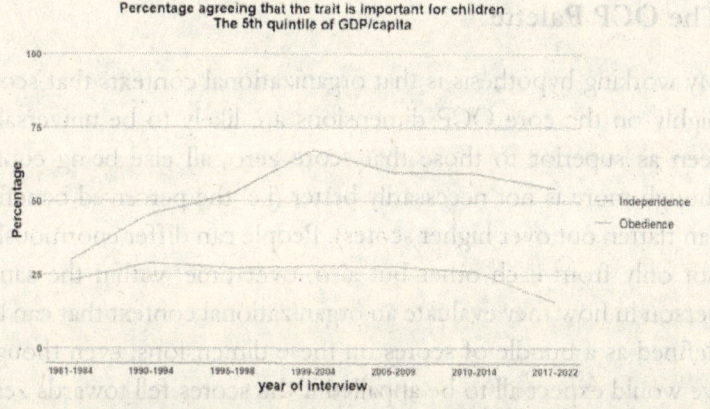

Figure 6a: The importance of independence and
obedience for children in the richest countries,
as reported in the World Values Survey

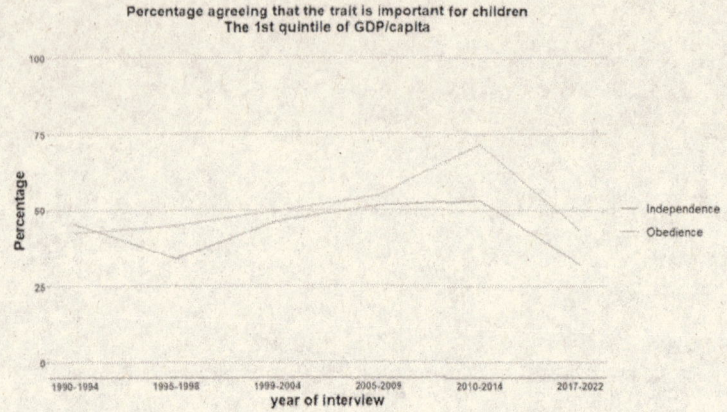

Figure 6b: The importance of independence and
obedience for children in the poorest countries,
as reported in the World Values Survey

So where Gen Z has grown up in conditions of higher economic
prosperity than their parents, we might see a greater preference
for autonomy in the organizational contexts they enter as adults,
but at least from this data, we cannot conclude that the demand
for greater autonomy is a universal Gen Z phenomenon.

The OCP Palette

My working hypothesis is that organizational contexts that score
highly on the core OCP dimensions are likely to be universally
seen as superior to those that score zero, all else being equal,
though more is not necessarily better (i.e. the perceived benefits
can flatten out over higher scores). People can differ enormously,
not only from each other but also, over time, within the same
person in how they evaluate an organizational context that can be
defined as a bundle of scores on these dimensions, even though
we would expect all to be appalled if the scores fell towards zero
on all dimensions without a compensating increase in pay and
material benefits.

Different types of organizations are likely to offer very different organizational contexts. The picture below is meant to illustrate the broad stroke differences in organizational contexts one might see between a traditional bureaucracy (Type I) versus other forms of organizing. Let's take two very different kinds of alternatives. The Type II context offers greater autonomy and opportunities to develop competence than the bureaucracy does. Type III offers greater relatedness.

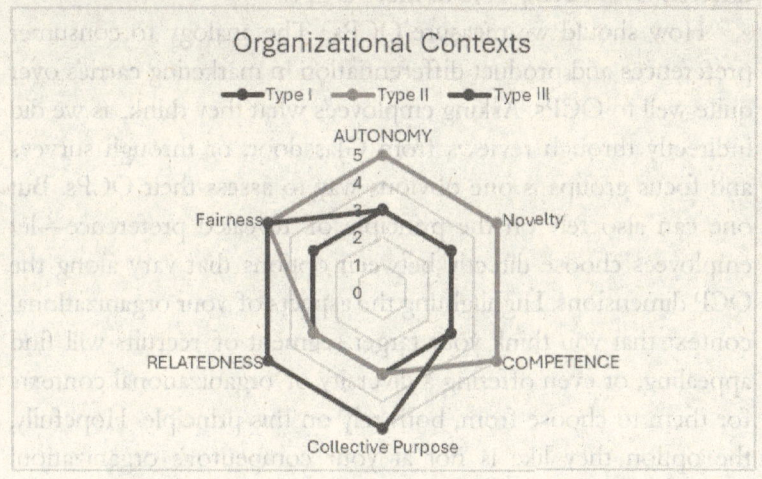

Figure 7: The key dimensions of organizational context preferences (OCPs)

I want to convey two ideas with this picture. First, unless you pay the most, you need to offer higher values on at least some dimensions and hope that there are enough people who value those dimensions highly enough to want to join and contribute. Figure 7 can also be interpreted as the weights that an individual places on the OCP dimensions, and the match between what the context offers and what the individual values is a source of motivation to the individual. This is how one differentiates and competes in a tight labour market for talent.

Second, there are multiple ways to offer appealing organizational contexts. For instance, cults offer relatedness, purpose, and fairness. Open-source communities don't necessarily do as well on the relatedness dimension, given the distributed and electronic interaction that characterizes them. However, they do satisfy preferences for autonomy, novelty, and competence in a way that cults do not. Neither pay salaries, but both succeed in attracting members. In other words, there are many ways to differentiate in being able to meet OCPs.

How should we measure OCPs? The analogy to consumer preferences and product differentiation in marketing carries over quite well to OCPs. Asking employees what they think, as we did indirectly through reviews from Glassdoor, or through surveys and focus groups is one obvious way to assess their OCPs. But one can also rely on the principle of revealed preference—let employees choose directly between options that vary along the OCP dimensions. Highlighting the aspects of your organizational context that you think your target segment of recruits will find appealing, or even offering a diversity of organizational contexts for them to choose from, both rely on this principle. Hopefully, the option they like is not at your competitor's organization! Revealed preference is not a perfect mechanism to match people to contexts as we will see in the next section, though it is a useful one.

Trade-offs in Organizational Context Preferences

We are now ready to take the last step in the argument. The most important payoff from thinking in terms of this universal six-dimensional palette of OCPs is that we can now be a lot more precise in assessing the impact of digitalization on human centricity. I propose that the **human centricity of an organizational context decreases when its members perceive a decline in**

one or more OCP dimensions that they care about, without a compensating increase in one of the other dimensions they care about. To keep the total compensation from material and nonmaterial sources constant, it is essential that a decline in human centricity is offset by an increase in pay. Additional monitoring efforts might also be required.

My definition allows us to see when a decline in human centricity in an organization has occurred, whether it is a problem and for whom. We can side-step the questions of whether an organization is currently human-centric or not, or even which one among two organizations is more human-centric (these would require us to make assumptions about thresholds on each dimension and comparability across organizations) but can focus instead on whether its human centricity is increasing or decreasing. Let's take an instance.

In 2015, *The Economist* published an influential article about 'digital Taylorism'.[48] The article explained how digital technologies had led to a renaissance in Frederick Taylor's ideologies of management: break complex work into simple modular chunks, ensure repeatability and monitor and measure as well as possible, link pay to performance (we will revisit these ideas in Chapter 5). In the cross hairs was Amazon, which was a pioneer in the use of these technologies. The article provoked a flood of outrage about this dehumanizing approach to managing workers. The approach was critiqued for taking the pleasure out of all work, reducing the scope for creative thinking by employees and, all in all, turning them into 'meatware'.

Viewed from the perspective of the OCP framework, this case illustrates two sorts of issues. First, what was the impact of these extreme monitoring technologies on other OCP dimensions such as fairness and competence? Greater measurement can produce greater transparency on the link between pay and performance, and more feedback on own performance. These could have increased perceptions of fairness and competence.

Could a hefty increase along these dimensions have compensated for any loss in autonomy and curiosity which was the focus of the article? We simply don't know because we don't have the data. It is theoretically possible that digital Taylorism creates a net increase in human centricity, which we would miss if we focused on only some of the OCP dimensions. To be clear, I am not arguing that Amazon became more human-centric by adopting its monitoring technologies, but that in general we cannot prejudge without data.

Second, a net decline in human centricity could be compensated for by an increase in salary. Employers need to pay more to reduce the human centricity of their organizations if employees have the capacity to freely leave and find other organizations that offer a better package in terms of a combination of human centricity and pay.[49] Even if employees are locked in and cannot easily leave to find other alternatives, the nature of work might still require intrinsic motivation if it is difficult to measure, monitor, and specify work.

While more material compensation cannot produce intrinsic motivation, by definition, it may produce greater effort even when effort is hard to measure and monitor, through a form of reciprocity: workers return the gift of higher wages with greater effort.[50] In fact, buried right near the end of the article was an interesting line—evidently Amazon's own employees did not seem to have a problem with being digitally 'Taylorized' as long as they got solid year-end bonuses. Economists call these 'compensating differentials'—unpleasant work needs to be better paid to attract workers. So even if these technologies did lower the human centricity of Amazon, perhaps they did so in a way that its employees did not care much about, given how they were getting paid. And if Amazon was happy paying higher salaries, presumably it was capturing enough value net of the higher salaries.

Put simply, digital Taylorism at Amazon *could* have been a 'win-win'. My point is not that it was—in fact, subsequent reporting and research suggests that many Amazon employees were dissatisfied and turnover was high, but Amazon relied on the high salary and benefits it offered to obtain a steady stream of fresh employees.[51] Rather, my point is that the OCP framework gives us a basic insight about human centricity in the face of digitalization: an organization designer should only decrease the human centricity of an organizational context (and therefore intrinsic motivation) in circumstances where: a) they can transform the nature of work in such a way that it becomes less reliant on intrinsic motivation— by increasing capacity to monitor, for instance; and b) they can afford to pay whatever compensating differential they need to pay their employees to offset the reduction in motivation.

In other words, unless they also simultaneously transform the nature of work in their organizations such that it is less dependent on intrinsic motivation (for instance, by making it more measurable, specifiable, and monitorable), taking any steps to reduce intrinsic motivation for employees will be costly for employers. This is why a decline in human centricity in an organizational context can be bad for both employees and employers. It does not guarantee an increase in pay for employees unless they have outside options, and even if they do increase pay, employers have no guarantee of effort from employees that is hard to measure and monitor.

The enhanced monitoring technology that Amazon deployed would seem to make intrinsic motivation less necessary, but the very fact that they had to pay higher than industry average bonuses strongly suggests that they had to compensate for not meeting OCPs. Possibly, they gained from new employees systematically failing to calibrate their own OCPs, so that while they would be drawn in by the high pay, eventually some would realize that their total compensation (net of OCPs) was unsatisfactory and would leave.

People may not be good at understanding their own OCPs, and the principle of revealed preference will not work well in this case. But for Amazon, as long as there was a steady stream of new employees, things just might have worked. This is not necessarily the only possible explanation for what happened at Amazon, but it is one that seems both internally consistent and covers all the facts.

I want to reiterate two broad points here: First, when assessing the impact of any new technology on the specific organization that adopts it, we should be concerned with the consequences for both goal and human centricity. One cannot really make sense out of situations like Amazon's without a careful consideration of the factors that underlie OCPs.

This argument does not detract from the potential value of protecting human centricity in organizations by other means such as increasing employee power through legislation. This can take the form of requiring board representation or shareholding rights for workers ('workplace democracy') or strengthening unions.[52] Rather, I wanted to outline an additional argument for why even purely goal-centric organization designers must nonetheless pay attention to human centricity. If nothing else, my argument may offer additional ammunition to legally empowered workers to articulate a rationale for the forms of human centricity they would like their organizations to have.

Second, in assessing the impact on human centricity, it could be useful to consider all the dimensions in the palette, and not anchor on one or two. For instance, a single-minded focus on increased autonomy might obscure effects on relatedness, competence, and fairness; an increase in autonomy may even lower effective material rewards for the risk averse. For others, it may lead to surprising indifference to poor pay, as seems to be the case for some gig workers.[53]

There may also be indirect effects to consider. For instance, hyper-monitoring is not the only way in which digital technologies can adversely affect autonomy. We find the extent to which companies monitor our 'digital exhaust'—through cookies, apps, our phones, and other digital devices—objectionable, not only because valuable private information (e.g. bank accounts) can be stolen, but also because those collecting this information can exploit us by being able to predict and shape our actions in ways we might not even realize.

The fact that we become quite predictable to those who possess this data may be sufficient grounds for unease, independent of additional concerns about mistrust in those who can make such predictions (would you be okay with your mother being able to predict your actions perfectly?). Simply being exposed to algorithms can undermine people's belief in their own capacity for autonomy. Having understood how AI works and recognizing the similarity to how humans work, it may be difficult for humans to maintain beliefs in strong forms of their own agency.[54] Much like Pinocchio, we may be forced to come to terms with our own strings.

The effects of AI algorithms on competence needs are both direct (e.g. humans may lose certain skills by having AI perform these) but also indirect—human skills may appear pitiful in an increasing number of domains when the benchmark is an AI. If algorithms proceed to redesign organizations to be more modular, or act as interfaces between humans to simplify their interactions, this can directly reduce relatedness. Indirectly, if our social interactions become heavily algorithm mediated (e.g. through avatars in the metaverse, or based on 'friend' recommendations), then the loss in authenticity may also harm relatedness.

Algorithms may directly harm fairness through algorithmic bias; but even if they are made unbiased, because their decisions are not fully understandable by humans, perceptions of unfairness may remain or increase. AI based recommender systems naturally curtail human exploration (compare browsing in a library versus Amazon's recommendations for a book).

Finally, the atomization of work that can be stitched together algorithmically, as many platforms ranging from Amazon Mechanical Turk (MTurk) to Uber do today, risks making a mockery of the sense of collective purpose.

Conclusion

My primary objective in this chapter was to offer a precise way of thinking about whether the adoption of algorithmic technologies in an organization is 'human-centric'. I proposed that we do this by looking at the impact on how the organizational context preferences (OCPs) of the organization's members are being satisfied (or not). This is important to do even if we are primarily concerned with goal centricity: the OCPs offer a framework for employers to strategically differentiate themselves in tight labour markets.[55]

My focus on human centricity comes from my belief that the immediate future of organizations is bionic, and not one of near complete automation (i.e. zero-human organizing). This does not rule out the possibility of the workforce within organizations shrinking. But even when that happens, there are more (and less) human-centric ways of managing that transition, which matter for both ethical reasons as well as pragmatic reasons involving the motivation of the employees who remain (and of those the organization hopes to hire in the future).

I have outlined a variety of ways in which the unthinking adoption of digital algorithms can harm the human centricity of organizations. Yet, I also believe that there are ways to use digital algorithms to organize in ways that can increase the satisfaction of OCPs. Much as bureaucracies can be enabling (by supporting workers to organize their own work) and not only coercive,[56] AI and other algorithmic technologies can be used to support organizational contexts that enhance autonomy, nurture relatedness, and offer opportunities for competence.

For instance, algorithms can be used to re-structure work so that outcomes become easier to observe, reducing the need to monitor behaviour, and therefore increasing the sense of autonomy. Relatedness can be enhanced by better matching between people when forming groups, using algorithmic technologies. The potential for algorithm-assisted training and feedback to enhance competence is already well recognized. In the succeeding chapters we will not only encounter instances such as these but also a general approach to organization design that makes it more likely to find applications of algorithmic technologies that are both goal- and human-centric.

PART II

HOW ALGORITHMS CHANGE ORGANIZATIONS

Chapter 4

Algorithms and Organizing

Objective 1: An organization must achieve its goals (i.e. it must be goal-centric).

Objective 2: An organization must provide a context that its human members find satisfying (i.e. it must be human-centric).

Problem Statement: Assess whether Algo X can improve the chances of attaining #1 without hurting the chances of attaining #2 (or vice versa).

Replace 'Algo X' with any digital algorithm you are considering adopting with the intention of changing how your organization works—collaborative work management tools, ERP systems, recommender systems, blockchain-based organizing, large language model-based assistants, or indeed AI in any form—and you have the core problem that this book is trying to help solve.

As I argued in Chapter 3, organizations that need to compete for talent that is intrinsically motivated towards the goals of the organization, cannot afford to ignore human centricity when adopting digital technologies. To operationalize this, I introduced a framework to think about the challenges of measuring and catering to organizational context preferences (or OCPs) (see Figure 7). In this chapter, I focus on goal centricity.

The impact of adopting new algorithmic technologies on goal centricity can be challenging to assess,[57] and one reason for this is that the impact is highly dependent on organizational practices.[58] Another important reason is 'hype', something that new technologies are particularly susceptible to. The market trends consultancy Gartner has captured a systematic pattern that new technologies seem to display—after a slow start and a ramp up in adoption, there can be a catastrophic decline in interest in the new technology.[59] Why is that? Because the initial peak came from 'inflated expectations', to be followed by the 'trough of disillusionment'. At the time of writing this book, technologies like generative AI are at the peak of inflated expectations, and we should not be surprised if there will be a fall-off in interest as many people discover that the technology does not come close yet to delivering on what has been promised.

The label 'hype cycle' for this pattern, which is how Gartner refers to it, is however somewhat misleading. It directs our attention too much to that initial peak of inflated expectations and how to avoid it. Equally important to bear in mind is that there can also be a gradual recovery as more careful adoption of the technology leads to a steady increase until it becomes pervasive. The strategic problem for managers is not only to avoid going in too early only to find themselves stuck on the peak of inflated expectations, but also to avoid standing by sceptically until well near everybody in the industry has already crossed the trough of disillusionment and they are left behind. In fact, having suffered from inflated expectations may increase the risk of abandoning the technology permanently and prematurely, thus losing out when it eventually becomes more pervasive. Much like a cat that touches a hot stove and then decides never to go near a stove again (forgoing milk), one can learn the wrong lesson from being burned at the peak of inflated expectations.

A systematic approach to understanding the implications of adopting a new technology for the goal centricity of an organization can help. This is the focus of this chapter. Drawing on research on organization design, I will describe the universal problems of organizing (UPO) framework. This approach treats *any* group with a goal as an organization, and highlights that regardless of the scale, scope, or history of an organization, its design always entails solutions to five universal problems.

Testing for the effects on goal centricity of the adoption of a new technology—or for that matter any organizational practice—amounts to understanding how these will affect the way these five UPOs are solved, and whether those solutions can enhance the capacity of the organization to attain its goals.

It is both possible and necessary today to take a data driven approach to testing if a new digital technology improves goal centricity. Too often in the past, organization design has been a matter of taste, opinion, and, frankly, superstition. The availability of granular data at scale can change that dramatically. However, the use of data to do organization design also raises troubling questions about privacy and control, bringing us, full circle, back to the question of human centricity.

A disquieting thought is that the current state of 'data-free' organization design, which is the norm, may perhaps represent the best balance we can strike between goal and human centricity in our organizations. I will argue against this view. I will preview here the challenges, which are considerable, and use the rest of the book to propose how we can address them.

The Universal Problems Of Organizing

Before we get into the details of how digital technologies affect the goal centricity of an organization, we need to become familiar with how organizations work—what their design is and does. Let's consider a few scenarios:

1. You've been asked to establish a new unit within your company, charged with swiftly developing and launching a suite of software applications for a newly emerging customer segment. This unit will comprise up to fifty individuals, drawn from both external hires and internal transfers. Where do you begin?

2. In a last-minute turn of events, you find yourself stepping in for a colleague to initiate preliminary discussions with a potential strategic alliance partner. Your mission is to establish a broad framework for collaboration between your company and the partner, aligning it with your objectives. With no prior experience in drafting alliance contracts, how do you proceed?

3. Your CEO expresses grave concern over your company's sluggish product development process compared to competitors. The development cycle, involving five distinct functions and three layers of managers, appears never-ending. She tasks you with investigating the root causes of this inefficiency. Where do you start?

4. Within an international organization, your responsibility is to coordinate multiple government agencies and private sector entities for an infrastructure development project. This represents your inaugural experience managing such a large, multi-partner consortium. What do you do?

5. You've just stepped in to replace the leader of an engineering team comprising eight highly educated, intelligent, and independent-minded employees. The CEO characterizes your team's project as a 'moon shot', with significant stakes and all eyes on you. However, you've never led a team before, let alone one pursuing a moon shot. How do you embark on this journey?

At first glance, these scenarios may appear as akin to each other as peas and peacocks. Some involve fresh initiatives (#1, #2,

#4), while others address pre-existing situations. Some involve external partners (#2, #4), others internal teams, and they range from small-scale (#1, #2, #5) to extensive undertakings (#3, #4). But look behind the curtain and you'll glimpse the same backstage dilemma: **How do we get a group to achieve a goal?** Whether launching a moon shot, building a new venture, coordinating an alliance or consortium, or aligning any team, you are solving organization design problems.

Current organization design thinking has moved far beyond the 'boxes and arrows' of organization charts.[60] Our conception of an organization now extends beyond traditional firms and government bureaus to encompass their components, such as teams, as well as the extensive networks in which they are embedded, such as platform-led ecosystems.

Instead, it's useful to think of an organization as any multi-actor system with a goal. This includes teams, departments, divisions, companies, strategic alliances, or entire platform ecosystems. A single large company may host a multitude of nested micro-organizations within its structure. For instance, in scenario #3, the individuals working in various functions of the company, trying to launch a new product, can be seen as an organization in themselves. Similarly, in scenario #1, the newly established unit you are orchestrating, or the team you are leading in scenario #5, or indeed the strategic alliance you are putting together in scenario #2 can all be regarded as distinct organizations. A collection of legally independent organizations can function together as a 'meta' organization, as in scenario #4—where each member in such a system can itself be a full-fledged legally distinct organization.

Why such an expansive concept of an organization? **Because regardless of differences in scale, scope, or sector, all organizations face the same universal problems of organizing (UPOs).** At a broad level, these can be summarized into two types of challenges: the division of labour and the integration of effort. Roughly, these correspond to the processes of 'breaking things down' and 'putting them back together'. Organizations fragment their activities into distinct tasks, allocated to various individuals and groups. Often (but not always) this is a consequence of specialization aimed at achieving efficiency. However, these fragmented activities must be harmoniously coordinated to attain the organization's goals.

We can dissect these further. The division of labour involves dividing the organization's overarching goal into sub-tasks (task division) and assigning these sub-tasks to individuals and groups (task allocation). Integration of effort entails addressing two interrelated sub-problems: motivating individuals through financial incentives and other means (reward distribution) and ensuring that they possess adequate information to do their own work and coordinate with others (information provision). Given that no set of solutions to these problems is likely to be perfect or permanent, we also need mechanisms for addressing exceptions and coming up with new solutions (exception management).[61]

When we embark on the (re)design of an organization with some goal (or strategy) in mind, we are always grappling with the same five universal problems of organizing:

Problem 1: What needs to be done (task division) given the goals of the organization?

If you are launching a new project, you will need to work this out, by reasoning backwards from the intended goals of the organization to the series of sub-goals and the tasks they entail. This includes the resource allocation necessary to support each task. Often, we can draw on our experiences from similar design problems we have already faced. If you want to organize a party with some friends, the task division is obvious from our past experiences: food, drinks, entertainment, invitations, clean up.

Suppose your team must build a new generative AI application to support product development? Now the task division is not so obvious. Sometimes we will have to make the best guess we can and iterate based on feedback.

Problem 2: Who should be responsible for each task (task allocation)?

Once we have broken down the goals of the organization into sub-goals and tasks associated with them, the next question is who is responsible for which of these? Task allocation must consider people's skills (what they are good at) as well as preferences (what they enjoy doing). It's clear the system analyst will talk to potential users of the generative AI application just as the deep learning expert will work on training the relevant model. It gets a little more complicated when people have multiple skills and strong preferences about what they want to do, which may not align with what they are skilled at. The deep learning expert may want to transition into a more user-facing role and would rather take on the role that the system analyst currently performs. Ignoring this preference can be demotivating for the individual. This pertains also to the next problem.

Problem 3: How should effort be rewarded to ensure motivation (reward distribution)?

The next challenge is how to get the people who have been assigned various sub tasks to execute them effectively. This requires motivation and some of that certainly comes from various forms of material rewards and resources as a share of the material output the group creates (e.g. salaries and bonuses). But as we have seen in Chapter 3, the satisfaction of organizational context preferences is another powerful set of motivators. Combining material and non-material rewards to produce a total compensation package that motivates people to deliver on their sub tasks is the essence of this challenge.

Problem 4: How can individuals be sufficiently informed to ensure competent and coordinated action (information provision)?

Even highly motivated people can fail to work effectively together because of coordination problems. Miscommunication, misunderstanding, and lack of synchronization are all hallmarks of the challenges that arise when people performing different tasks are not sufficiently informed, not only about how to perform their own task but also how to coordinate their work with others. This is why creating an appropriate flow of information in the system to get all parts to be sufficiently coordinated is the next crucial challenge.

Problem 5: What should be done when exceptions arise and we need new solutions (exception management)?

Once we recognize that the solutions that we come up with for the first four problems maybe neither perfect nor permanent, then we must recognize that we need a solution to handle exceptions—breakdowns in collaboration, possibly conflicts, arising between members of the group as they set about executing their respective tasks. For instance, if there isn't a clear allocation of responsibilities or if people are not sufficiently motivated or informed then problems in execution will surface. We might need to change the solutions to one or more of the other problems, in order to adapt to changes in the objectives or the environment of the organization.

   To resolve these exceptions (we can call them 'conflicts', bearing in mind that they need not involve people fighting or yelling at each other—subtle mistrust and a breakdown in harmonious cooperation and coordination will do), we may rely on centralization—one or a few individuals with authority to step in and make decisions on the fly and change things. This is what managers typically do— managers manage exceptions. When things are going by plan, we don't really need their active engagement.

But an alternative could be to seek new solutions through consensus. That's what decentralized, self-managed teams do. In either case, one needs to have a solution in mind for dealing with the inevitable exceptions as and when they arise.

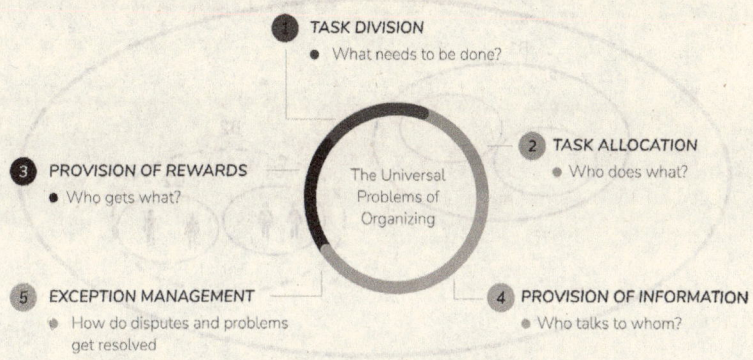

Figure 8: The universal problems of organizing

These five problems are universally relevant for *every* organization, whether it be a traditional manufacturing company, a cutting-edge technology start-up, a software development team, a sports team, or a musical quartet. They remain equally applicable when contemplating a comprehensive company-wide restructuring or when striving to enhance the efficiency of a particular team.

To see how this logic can be applied to organizations of any scale, let's start with a large group (e.g. A in Figure 9), in which each sub-group (B1 and B2) is treated as an actor. We will have to specify how tasks are divided and allocated among these sub-groups, how information and rewards are provided, as well as how exceptions and conflicts between sub-groups can be handled (by having a boss at level A who has authority over the people leading B1 and B2, for instance). The task allocation to B1 and B2 now become their respective goals in the next stage. We take each sub-group, B1 and B2, as an organization with its own goals (the tasks assigned to it in the previous stage) and repeat the same exercise of finding solutions to the UPOs, now treating sub-sub-groups C1 and C2 as actors. And so on till the relevant actors are individuals and we cannot go any further.

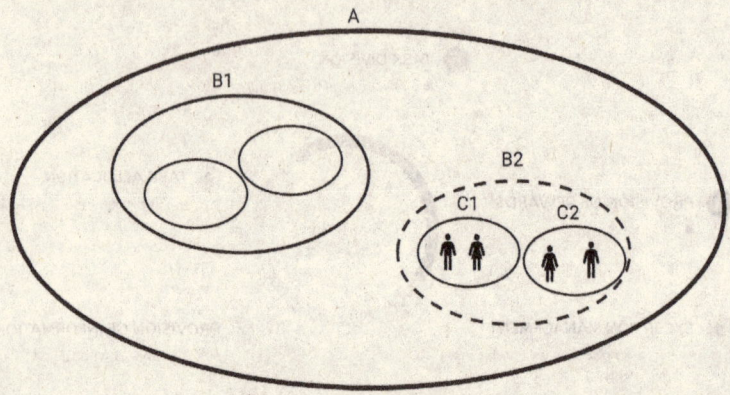

Figure 9: Cascading/nesting designs across levels

For instance, consider a large technology company undergoing a comprehensive restructuring. The process begins with the company defining its overarching goals and breaking them down into major tasks, which are then allocated to different divisions (e.g. B1 and B2 in Figure 9) such as product development, marketing, sales, and operations. Each of these divisions is then treated as its own distinct organization, with its own set of goals derived from the tasks assigned to it in the previous stage.

Consider the product development division as an example, which we can represent by B2 in Figure 9. It takes the tasks allocated to it and further subdivides them into smaller, more manageable sub-tasks such as research, design, and engineering. These sub-tasks are then assigned to different teams within the division (e.g. C1 and C2). The research team might be tasked with market analysis and user research, the design team with UX and

UI design, and the engineering team with the actual development of the product.

But the process doesn't stop there. Each team within the product development division is then treated as its own mini-organization. The engineering team, for instance, might further break down its tasks into front-end development, back-end development, and quality assurance. These tasks would then be allocated to individual engineers within the team. The front-end developer would focus on the user-facing parts of the application, the back-end developer on server-side logic and data management, and the QA expert on testing and ensuring the quality of the product.

In this way, the process of organizational design *cascades* down the hierarchy, with each level defining its goals, dividing tasks, and allocating them to sub-groups or individuals. Start-ups, as they grow, experience the process in reverse. As they expand beyond individual teams (like C1), they will have to define a super-group (B2) for *nesting* multiple teams like C1 and C2, and eventually as they get larger, all the way to A. Their challenge is to build-up, whereas when established companies reorganize, their challenge is to break down.

This cascading/nesting process is core to the approach that my colleagues and I have developed for understanding organization designs.[62] Its key insight is that every organization, regardless of its scale or how embedded it is within larger organizations (e.g. C1, B2, or A itself), faces the same universal problems of organizing. Their solutions may differ enormously across levels—C1 and C2 may be self-managing teams, but A may have a CEO, for instance. There may also be variations at the same level in the solutions used (by C1 and C2 for instance).

Nothing in Figure 9 is meant to indicate it is necessarily decentralized; the picture applies to both a traditional bureaucracy as well as new decentralized forms such 'holocracy' or decentralized autonomous organizations (which use 'sub-DAOs'). There can be much variation in how each organization solves its UPOs—in a centralized manner common in most firms, or a decentralized manner in organizations that promote self-management principles. Existing managerial tools like the balanced score card or the capital budgeting cycle also follow a cascading approach, though they focus on operational, not design decisions. More typically, design decisions (i.e. solutions to the UPOs), even for the smallest embedded organizations like C1 might be taken at the apex of A. In Chapter 8, I will discuss the problems with this approach and suggest an alternative.

Is the Design Working?

There are many metrics of performance we can use to assess if these five problems of organizing are being solved effectively, in a manner that promotes goal centricity. These will vary by context. Overall profit is too coarse a measure to rely exclusively on, as it may not be measurable for smaller units like C1 and C2 in Figure 9, and even for A, it depends on many things besides organization design (such as competition, strategy, and regulation). Much more often, we will look for metrics that stakeholders can use to assess how the organization is doing relative to its goals (e.g. how quickly an IT team responds to problems, how many patients recover after surgery, etc.).

Another class of metrics are measured internally within the organizational unit and are based on indicators of problems that signal poor underlying design. My collaborator Julien Clement and I have assembled a set of such indicators for use by practising organization design professionals. I reproduce this below, along with some suggestions on what the indicators might be telling us about poor underlying design, and how one might go about improving things. Be careful though! Fixing one problem can worsen another, because these are interconnected. More on that below.

Table 1: Metrics for diagnosing design effectiveness (Reproduction from *The Organizational Analytics E-Book*[63])

DESIGN PROBLEM	INDICATORS OF POOR-QUALITY SOLUTIONS TO THE PROBLEM	POSSIBLE SOLUTIONS TO CONSIDER
Task Division	• Conflicts due to overlapping and complex dependencies • Ripple effects with endless changes	• Modularize • Change the basis for clustering sub-tasks • Appoint somebody with authority to resolve conflicts • Build some slack into system • Allow self-selection into tasks • Training

Task Allocation	• Skill/capacity deficits • Idle time • Poor engagement • Shirking and freeriding	• Improve selection of members • Allow self-selection into tasks • Task reallocation • Appoint somebody with authority to resolve conflicts and monitor behaviour
Reward Distribution	• Gaming the measure • Fairness concerns • Risk burdens	• Review incentive systems • Allow self-selection into tasks • Appoint somebody with authority to monitor behaviour • Re-frame to invoke an alignment between individual and organizational goals

| Information provision | • Miscommunication and misunderstanding
• Failures of synchronization
• Skill deficits | • Review Information channels and systems
• Regrouping
• Build buffers and slack into the system
• Allow self-selection into tasks
• Training
• Appoint somebody with authority to resolve conflicts, direct behaviour |

Let's summarize the key ideas brought together in this approach to organization design based on the UPO framework.[64]

- An organization is any group with a shared goal. Large, intricate organizations can be understood as collections of nested, smaller micro-organizations.
- All organizations grapple with the same five universal problems. An organization's design constitutes a specific set of solutions to these five universal problems.
- The solutions include things that are directly controllable (e.g. structure and hiring) as well as more indirectly influenced (e.g. culture and networks). Ideally, these solutions must not only be mutually compatible (i.e. they exhibit internal fit) but also align with the organization's overarching goals and strategy (i.e. have external fit).

Uniquely, the UPO approach works in the same way across levels, from micro-organizations such as teams, committees, and departments to macro-organizations such as entire companies or ecosystems. We analyse all of them by thinking of them as organizations who must divide labour, integrate effort, and resolve exceptions and conflicts among their members.

Digitalization will not change the UPOs, though it will very likely change the menu of possible solutions to them. If we want to ask whether adopting Algo X will improve the goal centricity of our organization, we need to ask not only how it will change the characteristic of the product or service the organization delivers (e.g. will a predictive analytics technology lower costs of procuring raw materials) but also how it will change the way we solve the UPOs. It is well known that the aggregate effect on goal centricity of Algo X, measured by profits or productivity, will also depend on the way it changes how we organize.[65]

This is why it is important to ask, what exactly will that fancy new genAI application do to improve how your team works? Is it a good idea to build a new virtual community of practice within your company that interacts via VR? Or a decentralized autonomous organization using blockchains and other digital collaboration technologies? Or adopt a new digital platform for your online social movement that can lobby for better climate regulation?

In each case, you'll want to know how the technology (Algo X) you are considering will solve the UPOs (and if they do so better than current solutions). Can it chunk tasks better than what humans could do? Is it better at finding a match between what people can and want to do and what tasks need to be done? Will it change how people are rewarded through better measurement? Can it improve how they coordinate? And will it make it easier to detect and fix exceptions? In our subsequent chapters, we dig into the details of how different digital technologies shape how organizations function in a variety of ways, but we'll find that they *always* do so through how the UPOs are solved.

Even if the organization we are designing is a mix of humans and AI, it still needs to have solutions for the universal problems of organizing. In fact, even as we start building teams of AIs (which appears to be the next big development in generative AI) one thing we can be quite confident about is that these artificial organizations, to be goal-centric, will have to be designed keeping the same five universal problems of organizing in mind. Because these artificial agents will have different properties than human agents, the solutions needed will be different to those we deploy in human organizations. But these will be solutions to the UPOs.[66]

That is a powerful anchor of constancy in a rapidly transforming landscape.

Data-Driven Design

It seems inevitable to me that we will need organization-specific data to make well-informed decisions about adopting a new digital technology with the aim of improving the organization's goal centricity. This is true even for data-hungry versions of Algo X, such as modern AI technologies. Just because they use a lot of data, does not mean there is data that shows they can improve how we currently organize. There must be evidence even for evidence-based management, that it improves the status quo.

Let's consider a few alternatives, to see why I say this. First, we might simply adopt Algo X and hope for the best (that includes the hope that we can reverse our decision easily). This is such an obviously bad idea in most situations that I don't think I need to belabour the point that it should be avoided. Second, we might look at industry best practice. If other organizations around us are adopting Algo X and seem to be generating good results, then perhaps we should do likewise. While this sounds sensible, in practice it can be quite dangerous. We have talked about the risk of being taken in by hype. Further, the signals about the success of other organizations can be biased because they have an incentive to disguise their failures. Even if the signals are genuine, let's remember that just because something worked well elsewhere does not mean it will work for your organization. Given the skills and preferences of people in different organizations may be quite different, best practice for one company could be bad practice for another.

Third, we might place our faith in some framework or theory. Life would be simple if we could simply draw on some framework that could tell us exactly which design is appropriate for a given context, but alas, that is not to be. The practice of organization design does not become magically simple because there are only five universal problems. Even if each problem had only two possible solutions, we would still be looking at thirty-two possible designs (2 raised to the power 5). In practice, each of these problems of organizing can have multiple sub-dimensions, and along each dimension, multiple distinct solutions could exist. In any given situation, therefore, there may be thousands of design possibilities, what is called 'a large design space'.[67]

Not all designs in this space will perform equally well. If we imagine a landscape in which the height corresponds to performance, there will be peaks and troughs in this design space—many of each. And to make things interesting, we can't be sure if the peaks are next to each other. Step off a peak and you might make things better or worse, and it's hard to know without stepping off. This makes the design space 'rugged'. Our theories and frameworks can be helpful in identifying the dimensions of this space and may give us some hints about more-or-less promising regions, but I know of none that can tell us exactly where to go (that have any credibility).

The glib appeal to 'digital twins' as a solution also leaves me cold. A digital model of an organization *can* help us predict the impact of an organization design change, but only if the model is a good enough representation of the real organization, *as well as* the processes through which it can change. We have some way to go before we can build such models, though generative AI models appear to be getting better at simulating specific individuals.[68]

So how do we tame this complexity? Prior knowledge gained from research or practical experience can help define the dimensions for each problem and identify promising regions of the design space, but professionals and practicing managers cannot avoid having to verify what combinations work better in a particular context. It is a lot like drug discovery in the pharmaceutical industry, and for very much the same reason: the design space is vast and rugged, which is precisely what makes a combination of theory guided and data driven search valuable.

Theory and frameworks like the UPO can help guide our search for good designs, but we also need evidence—data—that allows us to make informed, contextually useful design decisions, such as how (and whether) to absorb Algo X. But not historical data from the past, because Algo X is new to your organization. Rather, we are talking about data from the future, the kind that tells you what is likely to happen when we adopt a design, to both goal centricity and human centricity. This is also called prototyping a design.

It simply involves trying it out to see if it works before adopting it.[69]

The Gold Standard (and an Alternative)

Field experiments, also known as randomized controlled trials (RCTs), are known as the gold standard for generating data to figure out if something works as claimed. These experiments involve randomly assigning some units (i.e. people, teams, projects, or departments) to a 'treatment' condition (the new policy or Algo X you're thinking of implementing) and others to the 'control group' (where things stay as they were without the new policy). A variant where we compare two treatments is called A/B testing. We then check if outcomes in terms of goal and human centricity are statistically different between the two conditions.

Randomization is crucial to this procedure. Imagine you implement, without randomizing, a new training policy and find that employees who applied for the training and attended it saw their performance improves. You have no way of knowing whether this is because your training was effective or because the people who applied for it are motivated, high performers whose evaluations were going to rise anyway. You might object that if you make the training mandatory for all employees you could just see if everyone's performance improves. But the problem is that you can't rule out other factors (industry cycles, demand spikes) that may have affected all employees. And this would be a rather costly way to find out that the training did not work!

Randomization ensures you avoid these problems by creating *counterfactuals*, that is, an understanding of what would have happened without the intervention. This is possible because randomized treatment and control groups are statistical twins: they are similar enough to be treated as identical, so the control group can serve as the counterfactual. We cannot establish causation without counterfactuals, and randomization is the best way we know of to establish counterfactuals (unless you have a time machine hidden away in your garage).

But randomization is also both costly and challenging. It is costly to implement because to get any sort of statistically meaningful data to analyse, sample sizes must be large.[70] The units being observed must be free of the influence of other units, and the treatment must be experienced identically by each unit in the treatment group.[71] Politically, you are taking a well-publicized risk that the new policy you are trying out will fail (if there was no such risk, what do we need the RCT for?). The pushback you will get from people who might think they have been unfairly assigned (or deprived of) participation in the treatment can be painful to manage too. And what you learn from even a perfect experiment conducted within sharply defined conditions for a limited period of time, may not hold true over longer time periods in the messy reality of business as usual, when people know they are no longer in an experiment being observed.

So, should we abandon the 'gold standard'? Not at all. Gold is nice to have, but hard to get. Rather we should be strategic about when to attempt it and use other approaches too. Randomization, when it can be applied, *is* the gold standard for providing counterfactuals, but the gold standard is not always necessary. We can attempt to construct counterfactuals from other kinds of data—try to make a well-informed guess about what might happen if we were to adopt Algo X, and that guess might be enough to learn something useful. After all, I seriously doubt our ancestors discovered fire or the wheel through randomized control trials! Instead, very likely, they relied on trial-and-error learning (aka experiential learning)—another powerful engine that produces data.

At its core, trial-and-error learning, also known as learning-by-doing and experiential learning consists simply of doing things, observing the outcome, and repeating the action if it seems satisfactory, else trying something else. If this sounds absurdly simple, it is. Even pigeons can do it. But AI algorithms that underlie self-driving cars and large language models also rely on the same principle (in their world, it is called 'reinforcement learning'). The sophistication lies in how carefully one observes actions and outcomes (i.e. captures and maintains good records of practices and performance), what one learns from it (i.e. think about counterfactuals by considering what changed and what was constant across trials) and how we choose and implement the next action. In fact, one of the most actively researched areas in organization science is concerned with how individuals and groups learn from the data generated by experience and how they can do so more effectively. Here are some of the insights that have emerged, some quite surprising:

- *Pay close attention to what you did, not just how it turned out.* Good data on what actions we took and what outcomes we observed is crucial to effective experiential learning. This is what experimentation in a controlled setting amounts to—to have good data on what we changed and what we held constant and how the outcome changed. For instance, if you want to trial a new AI powered tool to help your team improve their effectiveness, it is not enough to just observe whether performance improved (since this is not an RCT). You must also have good records of what people actually did with the technology— how it was used and how it changed the way the UPOs were being solved. This might seem obvious, but most organizations historically have not been good at keeping such records, at least in part because those who decide are not often the ones who do.[72] Managers may make decisions, but subordinates implement them, and the implementation may or may not reflect exactly what the managers had in mind.

- *Occasionally try some actions at random, without good reasons.* Suppose you believe doing A is better for you than doing B. Therefore, sensibly, you do A and find the outcome to be what you expected. Your beliefs are strengthened about the wisdom of doing A instead of B. But should they be? Maybe not. It is possible that in fact your views about B are biased—it would have been better to do B. But you did not, and you will never know. Your biased beliefs about B being inferior to A are self-confirming because acting on these beliefs prevented you from discovering they are false. To escape biases in one's thinking, it is therefore important to do things that seem counter-intuitive given our current beliefs.[73] Pretty sure that the Algo X variant is better for you than Algo Y? Nevertheless, it may not be a bad idea to run a small pilot with Algo Y. With new technologies, often our confidence about how well they will work may exceed our competence at being able to evaluate them, as the hype cycle shows.

- *Learn from others.* We know that it is useful to exchange experiences with others who are also learning through trial and error, even if the problem they are working on is not exactly the same as our own. This is one reason why communities of design practice can be very powerful. How is this different from copying best-practice? The answer lies in the word 'trial'. A trial is a small-scale or temporary attempt, not a commitment to a course of action; it is reversible. We should learn from the trials of others to construct our own trials, not copy their actions as if they are the best practice possible for us.[74] Many organizations have been building internal communities around the usage of AI tools that span functions and geographies, and these have been quite helpful in generating insights about what tools work and what do not in their context.

- *Authority, centralization, and an imposed common vision can all be good for learning.* When many interlinked units must engage in trial and error together, the feedback each receives is partly a function of what actions others are taking. It turns out that having an aligned vision to begin with, even if incorrect, is better than a diversity of viewpoints (even if some of them are correct).[75] Further, organizing this group in a hierarchical manner, with a single individual influencing others more than they influence him, can improve trial and error learning even if that individual has no superior insight or capacity for monitoring.[76] Why? Because the alignment makes it easier to learn from the feedback. If we all know what actions each of us take and interpret the feedback in the same way, we will collectively learn more from it. Leader-led, highly aligned teams that are engaged in interdependent work can be agile, because they can learn from feedback in a more coordinated way.

What is common to these insights is that they all suggest ways to improve the quality of our counterfactuals so that we can maximize what can be learned from our experiences. Put simply, 'controlled' and 'trial' are still useful concepts for experiential learning, even if we don't have the 'randomized' bit.

Ethical Use of Data

I have advocated strongly for the use of data in organization design, having launched the first Organizational Analytics course for MBAs and the first programme on AI for senior executives at INSEAD. I even co-wrote (with Julien Clement) a free e-book about data driven organization design.[77] But my enthusiasm has always been tempered by worries about the ethical use of data. Students have sometimes been puzzled by my apparent ambivalence on the topic—was I telling them that data could be used to improve how organizations work or was I not?! I've tried to explain my discomforts in various ways, but I believe they can be crystallized in the language developed in this book: I do not want to see data being used to improve goal centricity of organizations while harming their human centricity.

To make this concrete, consider the amount of digital data that organizations now have about their employees, gathered as 'digital exhaust' from platforms like Teams, Outlook, Slack, Zoom, and now Copilot. This is clearly a bonanza for analysts. Before these platforms existed, there was no system to capture, for example, informal networks of influence that may determine a strategy's success or failure, or the decline in morale preceding a wave of resignations (surveys as sources of this kind of data have never been very satisfying). Companies now face an explosion of data about nearly everything employees do, from the emojis they exchange to the length of their lunch breaks and the questions they ask GPT. We live in bionic organizations (Chapter 2), remember? Add machine-learning algorithms and A/B testing to the mix, and we are looking at unprecedented capabilities to do rigorous, data-driven design.

But these capabilities also raise troubling ethical questions. These extend well beyond the problem of biases in data being reproduced if the data is used mindlessly. If your managers and HR department are prejudiced against some types of people, who are rarely promoted, using data on promotions to forecast whom to hire or promote will perpetuate these prejudices. This is not news any more thanks to several thoughtful critiques,[78] and de-biasing and fairness metrics have become a part of the AI lexicon, even if we are far from perfecting solutions.

Rather, the concerns I am flagging here are organizational-level reflections of equally troubling questions at the societal level.[79] At what point does the use of organizational data cross the line between useful and creepy? To get my students to think about this, I run the following thought experiment in my classroom. It's called 'Say when'.

I'm now going to describe a number of use cases of data for improving employee retention. As you know, this is a domain where data application to organizational effectiveness has taken off. I'll list the use cases in an order that I think will make you increasingly uncomfortable, so be warned! You have to raise your hand to say 'stop' at the use case that makes you uncomfortable. Please keep your hand up till the end of the exercise once you raise it.

Note, every single use case I am describing is technically feasible today. It is even perfectly legal in many legal jurisdictions. Ready?

1. Using data, we can tell what factors make employee departure more likely (e.g. tenure, time since last promotion, gender).
2. Using the same data, we can forecast that the probability of a particular individual, Ann, quitting this year is very high.
3. Adding email traffic network data, we can estimate that Arif who is a regular email correspondent of Ann will quit with a high probability if Ann quits.
4. Using text data from Slack channels and in company emails, we can use natural language processing (NLP) to gauge that Anil and Shanaya seem most disengaged and at high risk of departure.
5. Using video images from official Zoom calls, we can detect that Bob tends to be aggressive towards his female co-workers and is causing high rates of exit among women in his teams.

Nearly every hand is up by the time I get to #4 and beyond. But it is interesting for the participants to also observe that they differ from each other in their stopping points.

We do not yet have a globally agreed framework on regulating the use of data and AI technologies, but the European Union (EU) has made considerable progress towards both. The EU's AI Act[80] is a remarkable document, with a lot of thought put into issues of data privacy and ethical use. It is by no means perfect but given that most other jurisdictions do not even have an equivalent, the EU's AI Act deserves respectful attention, at the very least. I do know of colleagues who will argue that no regulation is always superior to imperfect regulation, but this seems to me an ideological argument that I do not see much point in engaging with.

The EU's guidelines are quite detailed when it comes to distinguishing levels of risk, and by my reading make every use case beyond #1 above illegal. Also by my reading, practices such as behavioural 'nudging' are incompatible, in spirit if not in the letter, with these guidelines. If you are operating in the EU, this Act is what will shape your most basic design choices about how digital technology can be applied to how organizations work. If you operate elsewhere, you should ask yourself why you (or your organization's leaders) would not voluntarily choose to abide by these standards too. There is certainly the risk, to be carefully managed, that the regulations curtail the speed of innovation, but innovation is not an end in itself; it must be in the service of human welfare, and the AI Act makes this salient.

Beyond what is required by regulation, there are some basic 'good hygiene' practices that organizations must think about, such as setting up human data governance guidelines. Sensible principles include:

- **Choice:** Did the individuals whose data you intend to use have a say in whether you could do so? Choice could be established through notice, the right to opt-out or in, or explicit consent. (In the EU, explicit consent is essential.)
- **Cloaking:** Have you taken steps to anonymize, pseudo-anonymize, or aggregate the data to prevent (involuntary) leakage during analysis phase? Has the analyst given the necessary undertakings to protect the data from leakage and misuse?

- **Curation:** Do you have data secured in a safe environment? Have you restricted access on a need-to-know basis? Is the data accurate? Have you considered the duration for which the data will be stored and when it will be deleted?
- **Circulation:** Have you ensured that the results are only circulated to those specified when establishing choice?

These principles take cognizance of two relevant elements of organizational context preferences we discussed in Chapter 3, namely autonomy and fairness. Data privacy is not only a matter of reputation or embarrassment; it is fundamentally about the need for autonomy—to be free of the control and influence of others who have access to data about you, possibly without your even being aware of it. Data quality (and privacy) also affect fairness of outcomes.

Instead of thinking about data governance as a compliance issue, organizations might think about how they manage their employee's data to compete to attract and motivate talent through meeting OCPs. Employees who place a high weight on autonomy and fairness, for instance, might find it more appealing to work in an organization that has explicit policies that give employees control over how their data is used.

Organizations can also borrow a useful institution from universities. When I or my colleagues want to conduct analysis using data on people—students, colleagues, or even those recruited from outside the university—we must have our research proposal evaluated by what is called an Ethics Review Board. (In some places it is called an Institutional Review Board.) Every proposal is vetted by such a board and examined for the trade-off between possible harm and gain in knowledge. It's not always easy for these boards to do their work and researchers can become frustrated with how slow or tedious the evaluation process can be. (I've been in that camp, too, sometimes.) But I doubt many of us practicing social scientists would argue that the review board process should be discarded. In a similar way, any use of data to make decisions that affect people within the organization for the purposes of organization design could usefully be examined by an internal Ethics Review Board that an organization might set up.

Conclusion

In this chapter, I have discussed a variety of ways in which we can ensure human-centric uses of data to design goal-centric organizations, as well as assess how new digital technologies will affect the balance between goal and human centricity. Controlled trials (with and without randomization) can help us determine how a new digital technology will affect the way an organization works—how the universal problems of organizing are solved in that specific organization.

The use of data in this process is essential. Its use should adhere not only to regulatory guidelines but also to ethical guidelines. Ethical review boards within organizations can help, not just to ensure ethical standards are upheld but also possibly as a centre of competence in designing and analysing data from controlled trials. Yet, they represent traditional solutions in the sense that the responsibility for ethical use of data is entrusted to a few (powerful) individuals.

In Chapter 8, I will describe an approach to organization design that offers a radical alternative—to let people who must live and work in a design participate in selecting that design, based on data they are comfortable using, and supported by algorithms in making these choices.

Chapter 5

Digital Division of Labour

The image is black and white, and somewhat jerky. The little man in the overalls is tightening bolts on an assembly line as rapidly as they come through—with a rhythm that matches the comedic music in the background. Next to him stands another worker, doing something equally repetitive and mind numbing. Sometimes the little man gets out of synch—when a fly alights on his nose, for instance. Chaos ensues as his downstream neighbour struggles desperately to keep the rhythm of work going. It's all very funny. But also, quite horrible.

If you have not seen Charlie Chaplin in the 1936 film *Modern Times*, you have missed one of the finest and most savage critiques of the dehumanizing effects of organizing. The narrowly defined tasks, performed repetitively in lockstep with everybody around you doing the same, and all of it monitored relentlessly—this is an organization that a sadist might take pride in having designed.

Any group with a goal, namely an organization, must figure out solutions to the universal problems of organizing (Chapter 4). Of these, the first two—task division and task allocation—together constitute the division of labour. What needs to be done, and who does what? As an organization designer you need answers to these questions whether you're organizing a party, launching a new product, building a startup, or creating a consortium of different agencies to deliver a mega project. That's how we together divide up and conquer goals that would be unthinkable to attain as individuals, and that's all that the 'division of labour' fundamentally is.

How did we go from there to Chaplin's grotesque (yet realistic) portrayal of the mind-numbingly repetitive activities that factory workers have had to endure? Is that journey inevitable?

Or is it possible to do division of labour without turning organizations into machines and people into cogs? Can digital algorithms help?

To answer these questions, we will have to dive deeper into the fundamentals of the division of labour. Hold tight.

The Curse of Specialization: Part 1

If you take the phrase 'division of labour' to mean literally what it says—how to divide up the work ('labour') needed to be done among the members of the group—then there are many possible ways of doing it. In fact, if you have n tasks and m people in a group then you have n^m possible divisions of labour. The many possible divisions of labour based on specialization are just *some* of them.[81]

By convention, the grandparent of the idea of specialization is held to be Adam Smith. Consider the original example provided by Smith in 1776: Pin making could be divided into 'eighteen distinct operations, which, in some manufactories are all performed by distinct hands, though in others, the same man will sometimes perform two or three of them.'[82]

In Smith's highly cited account, he describes three benefits of the division of labour in the pin factory—the improved productivity of the worker, the saving of time lost in switching tasks, and the development of new methods of working (including mechanization) arising from specialization. Organization design theorist Henry Mintzberg noted that at the root of all three benefits cited by Smith is the repetition of a set of tasks that requires similar inputs of skill and effort.[83] This narrows down the scope of what the worker needs to think about—it focuses attention. The repetition also means that the fixed cost of learning how to do this one thing very well can then be amortized over many repetitions. The benefits of specialization thus depend fundamentally on repeating a narrow range of activities again and again. For any significant scale of production, the benefits of specialization are most likely to accrue if we can chunk up the work so that it consists of tasks that can be repeated.

Let's take an example. Suppose you and your team of three helpers had to do some carpentry—make a small dining table and three chairs. To get the benefits of specialization, you should divide the tasks involved in such a way that each person can perform the same few activities with as many repetitions as possible. You would divide up the activities of cutting, sawing, nailing, finishing, painting, and polishing among yourselves, since each piece of furniture entails all these activities. The person doing the cutting would be able to repeat this activity many times, the person doing the nailing would as well, and so on.

The technical term for this is 'activity-based task allocation' since each activity is performed by a different person. This could produce quite skilled experts at cutting, nailing, polishing, etc. by the time we are done. In a way, it's a minor miracle! If we can divide up the objectives of a group into fine-grained tasks such that members of the group perform a small number of highly repeatable tasks each, then even if they began with no skill for any task, over time they would develop it and become experts. They would become 'specialists'.

If we had to build not one set of dining furniture but a dozen, the gains from specialization would be even greater. Greater scale means more potential for repetition, and that in turn means more benefits from all that repetition entails. Your team gets more productive, the furniture improves in quality, and your costs from waste and mistakes go down. You can now outperform other teams of furniture makers! Happy customers abandon them and flock to you, and your scale of production increases. Soon you are hiring more (specialist) workers . . .

There is just one problem. To chunk up work into extremely thin slices, it is necessary for the work to be 'decomposable', by which we mean that the parts are sufficiently independent so that we don't end up creating a gigantic coordination problem. The cutting and sawing of the wood need to be aligned so that the pieces can be nailed together accurately by somebody else. When things don't fit, there will be plenty of blame and anger to go around. When you were four people, a lot of that coordination and conflict resolution could occur informally, with some good-natured bantering. Now with forty, mostly strangers, it can become a nightmare.

So, the problem created by specialization is that it ramps up the need for coordination. But if you can sort that out by putting in place procedures and people who specialize in monitoring and coordinating, then the gains in productivity can be astounding. Having a few people dedicated to acting as central points of coordination across all the specialists—**to embed some centralization into the system**—allows for specialization despite interdependencies.

We have a name for these individuals who produce centralized coordination among specialists, who step in to sort out exceptions and smooth over conflicts. They are called 'managers'. Since there are limits on how many people a single manager can oversee (the technical term is 'span of control'), we set up multiple layers of managers as we scale up production, and we call that a 'hierarchy'. The apex manager at the top exercises centralized control (to varying degrees) over the rest.

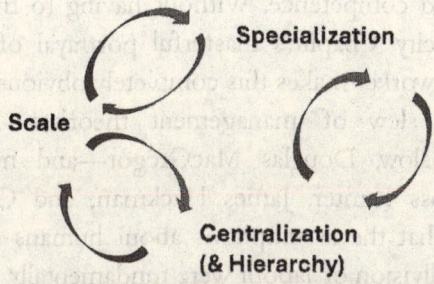

Figure 10: Scale, specialization, and centralization
reinforce each other

This mutually reinforcing dynamic between scale, specialization, and centralization (see Figure 10) is an idea that is today strongly associated with Frederick Winslow Taylor, but the core ideas were already present in the writings of classic management theorists who came before him (such as Henry Fayol, for instance). Taylor formalized the idea and combined it with an engineering sensibility of optimization and measurement, to produce the division of labour based on specialization and accompanied by the intensive measurement and monitoring that Chaplin was to eventually parody.

But why do we intuitively recognize Chaplin's portrayal as sophisticated critique, and not just some plain old slapstick? ('Not that there's anything wrong with that', as Jerry Seinfeld would say). I believe it is because Chaplin managed to show just how antithetical to human centricity the system based on specialization, scale, and centralization had become in the Taylorist factory. Working individually on narrowly defined tasks that lack any clues about how they contribute to an overall purpose with a high degree of repetition and under continuous monitoring is *literally* the opposite of what one would do if you wanted to create an organizational context that met basic preference for relatedness, autonomy, and competence. Without having to theorize about human centricity, Chaplin's masterful portrayal of the hapless assembly line worker makes this completely obvious.

A whole slew of management theorists—Elton Mayo, Abraham Maslow, Douglas MacGregor—and more recently Rosabeth Moss Kanter, James Hackman, and Greg Oldham pointed out that the assumptions about humans embedded in the Taylorist division of labour were fundamentally flawed. Many rediscovered the work of Mary Parker Follett, a contemporary of Taylor, who had proposed a very different approach to organizing, which was explicitly human-centric. These pioneers started an arc of research that has brought us to the point where I believe we can now state precisely what organizational context preferences are.

As I described in Chapter 3, besides compensation, benefits, and other material rewards, we know that people value autonomy, a sense of connection to others (relatedness), and the ability to feel that they are competent and mastering what they are doing. They also value being treated fairly, they enjoy novelty and seek a sense of meaning and collective purpose in the work that they do. Not everybody weighs all dimensions equally and there are enormous variations across cultures and within them as well. But few people would be indifferent to setting the scores on all these dimensions down close to zero, and that's exactly what the extreme forms of Taylorism did.

While describing the ant colonies he spent a lifetime studying, the biologist E.O. Wilson wryly remarked that communism was a great idea, but we had applied it to the wrong species: it might have worked better for ants than humans. In a similar spirit, one might say Taylorism is a good idea for organizing based on hyper-specialization, but for the wrong species.

In fact, experts in human pre-history believe that high levels of specialization is a recent phenomenon, and that there was far less of it in the hunter-gatherer groups our ancestors lived in.[84]

I believe we can make a case for specialization to be included in that list of Promethean discoveries—along with agriculture and atomic fission—that have created a lot of value for our species but also a lot of misery.[85]

With specialization, we set out to divide and conquer, and may in the process have been divided and conquered.

Alternatives to Specialization

Division of labour based on 'activity-based task allocation' and specialization is not the only possibility for our little furniture shop. An alternative could be 'object-based task allocation', where we might ask each helper to make an entire object—a chair each—and you make the table. In many ways, it is the more intuitive way to divide labour: we see objects all the time, but we must imagine the activities that lead up to them.[86] With this division of labour, each worker would undertake all the steps and sub-tasks such as cutting, sawing, nailing, finishing, and polishing (once each) to make their item of furniture. There would be far less repetition of activity in this case, of course. This would also mean we would have to give up on all those benefits of repetition that specialization produces, such as an increase in productivity and less time lost in switching between tasks. So why would we ever consider this alternative seriously?

In my original story, at some point I turned you into a sort of Henry Ford of dining tables. But suppose instead we were doing things at smaller scale. A one-off project for making dining furniture (or any one-off project, for that matter) will not have as much scope for repetition of activity and therefore for building up specialization. Bespoke work does not benefit as much from specialization.

Another general reason for considering object-based division of labour arises whenever it is very hard to decompose tasks.

Suppose it is difficult to monitor and coordinate the work of specialists in cutting, sawing, and polishing, which need to be closely aligned to each other; it might be easier to assign all these tasks to the same person, who can after all coordinate best with themselves. It may also be easier to just measure and evaluate the final product (a chair or a table), rather than monitor and supervise the activities that produce it. Lower interdependence between the work being done by different people makes the work more modular—it breaks down into chunks with weak dependencies between them but strong linkages within. This also means less need for centralized control to ensure coordination across people, since they do not need to coordinate as much.

Primarily, object-based division of labour creates advantages through allowing more attention to the dependencies between the distinct tasks needed to produce an object (i.e. customization), by allocating all such activities to one person or a group of closely interacting people. In our furniture example, this is the case where each worker produces an entire chair or table, end to end. This kind of division of labour prioritizes coordination among the tasks needed to produce an object, at the expense of ignoring opportunities for specialization by tasks that are common to different objects.

Further, when the objects don't need to be made in sequence (e.g., the table can be made before or after the chair) one might also be able to save time by working in parallel.

If this sounds familiar, it might be because you have recognized the underlying logic separating functional from product- or geography-based divisional groupings in large companies—it is the same picture on a larger canvas. When a company such as Procter and Gamble (P&G) organizes itself by functional departments such as R&D, manufacturing, and sales (and P&G used to be organized this way in its early years), they're going after the benefits of specialization. When instead they organize themselves by product divisions, one for soaps, one for detergents, etc., then they're going for the gains from customization. The benefits of one approach become the opportunity costs of the other. The fact that large companies often shuffle between these arrangements is one of the strongest pieces of evidence we have that gains from specialization don't always win.

But in addition to all these benefits, where object-based division of labour really distinguishes itself from activity-based approaches is that it is more human-centric. It escapes many of the most dehumanizing effects of specialization brought about by the individual having to repeat a narrow range of activities, with no clear links to a final purpose, and be monitored closely to ensure coordination with others doing the same. It meets our preferences for novelty, a sense of meaning in what one is doing, and autonomy.

To summarize, in the activity-based approach, we get gains from specialization by pursuing repeatability of tasks that apply to all objects (e.g. sawing, polishing) but will need to worry about how to coordinate these tasks if they are highly interdependent; centralized coordination is the typical solution. In the object-based approach, we instead get the gains from customization (e.g. the entire chair is made by one person, or a group of people work closely together to make something), where the coordination among tasks needed to produce an object can be excellent, but we might lose out on the possible gains from repetition and specialization by consolidating the tasks that are common across objects. But the object-based approach may have an edge when it comes to human-centric work design in no small measure because it diminishes the need for centralized coordination.

Digital Taylorism Revisited

To the extent that humans want things other than material compensation from their workplace, the division of labour advocated by Taylor does not work well for human organizations, particularly when intrinsic motivation is crucial to productivity. I believe Taylor himself understood this quite well. His 'scientific management' principles relied heavily on the idea of standardized sequence of actions, and the ease of observing whether the sequence was being conformed to. Why? Because the more perfectly one can specify and measure a worker's actions, the less important their intrinsic motivation (and therefore the need to satisfy OCPs) becomes for productivity.

But even setting aside the dubious ethics involved, this approach becomes untenable as the proportion of production that occurs in the worker's mind increases. It's hard to observe a knowledge worker and tell if they are working or shirking; we must wait for the results. This is why Taylorism is not the dominant mode of organizing any more. This is not to say that it has disappeared from our landscape—it lives as much in sweatshops in poor countries as in fast-food chains in the richer ones. But it has most certainly been in retreat in the knowledge economy.

Until recently. In Chapter 3, we encountered the influential concept of 'Digital Taylorism'—a renaissance in Frederick Taylor's approach to organizing using digital technologies: break complex work into simple modular chunks, ensure repeatability, monitor and measure as well as possible, and link pay to performance. An important concern with algorithmic technologies is that they can boost each of these practices, and Amazon's warehouses seem to have been ground zero for the birth of this new variant on an old theme.

There are certainly places in the economy where algorithms can slice the work that humans do ever finer, to extract greater gains from specialization by the humans engaging repetitively in the same tasks. Crowdsourcing platforms for micro-tasks like Amazon MTurk use algorithms to divide large tasks (such as image tagging and data entry) into smaller, well-defined micro-tasks. These can then be undertaken by a large pool of human workers remotely, leveraging their specialized skills (e.g. specific language knowledge, image recognition ability). Gig working platforms like Uber operate similarly, parsing ride and food delivery activities finer and letting humans specialize in the service fulfilment alone, and automating order taking, billings, and customer feedback. Even the manual work in warehousing could be reengineered in this way, as Amazon's reported attempts suggest.

It is important to distinguish whether one is drawing in new entrants into the labour pool to take on this sort of gig work (as with Uber) or is instead converting existing work conditions into a hyper-Taylorized version (as in Amazon). In the former, there is at least the redeeming feature of providing potentially new employment opportunities for some, whereas in the latter, it is a straightforward contest between goal centricity and human centricity.

Sometimes the two processes are linked by the force of competition. When platforms offer gig work for a variety of services that might have been done by in-house employees, eventually there may be no in-house employees left and they too might be forced to operate through gig platforms.

Gig work thus raises a complicated set of issues and we do not yet have a good way of assessing what the aggregate effects for human welfare have been. Sometimes, even gig workers themselves may not be very clear on whether they are benefiting or being exploited.[87] While gig work offers a path into the workforce for many and offers additional income with some flexibility on when and how much to work, it offers none of the positive aspects of traditional full-time work, such as stable pay, benefits, social connection, and opportunities for career progression. It may even have taken away these benefits from full-time employees who find themselves made redundant as their employers switched to rely on gig workers.

All that said, I am not convinced that digital Taylorism is the most important challenge we face in keeping organizations human-centric in the algorithmic age. Why? Because there is a natural limit to the hyper specialization that digital Taylorism can impose on humans. Once we get to a point where tasks have been so finely carved apart so that what remains is both simple and amenable to repetition, it's no longer clear why a human must do what remains. Ride sharing and food delivery still have large components that require manual dexterity, but for many varieties of knowledge work that involve micro-tasks, there isn't much human future left for the highly repeatable, extremely simple task. Image labelling and transcription are forms of work close to hitting this limit.

Put simply, digital Taylorism seems to be a path headed towards full automation, with poor work conditions for humans being a 'mere' way station. Odious enough as this is, there is however a different sort of danger from algorithms and specialization, one which does not involve saddling humans with boring, repetitive work, but rather claims to free them from it.

There is a genre of writing in recent years that extolls the virtues of humans and AI algorithms, collaborating in a manner that entails specialization *between* them, with humans handing over some of the sub-tasks they previously did to algorithms, but possibly retaining some oversight. Relying heavily on the language of 'win-win', the subtle, almost ingratiating pitch is to allow machines to augment us by 'collaborating' with us.[88] Let algorithms take on the boring routinized work (that in any case they can do better than humans), and let humans specialize in all the noble, ineffable work that makes us human. Or so the argument goes.

On the surface, this is of course nothing but the logic of relative advantage that Adam Smith recognized long ago in the pin factory. It is also the logic that underlies international trade, outsourcing, and strategic alliances: if each party specializes in what they do best, both can be better off through gains from trade.

But there are two insidious aspects to this argument that we should pay a little more attention to: first, for what kind of tasks do algorithms truly have an advantage over us? And second, what are the long-term consequences of specialization between humans and AI, on humans?

The Curse of Specialization: Part 2

When we collaborate with an AI based on the logic of specialization, this implies that there are certain tasks that we used to do that we now pass on to the machines because they have a relative advantage over us at those tasks (which could be absolute or comparative). The widely held view, till very recently, has been that it is routinized work that is prone to takeover by algorithmic automation and that non-routinized work remains a human prerogative. One can almost imagine a sort of anti-Taylorist utopia, with the repetitive, narrowly defined work that humans would have done in Taylorist systems now taken over by machines.

So, what exactly is routinized work? Some characteristics people associated with the term include 'repetition', 'simple', 'codifiable', and 'involving low levels of creativity'. However, I believe that apart from 'repetition', none of the other adjectives accurately describe the limits of what AI algorithms can do today.

It *is* true that if a task is repetitive, the economic incentives for automating it can go up, because the variable costs of machine execution can often be lower than human execution (even if the fixed costs are higher). Further, the amount of data accumulated on the task will also likely be large for a repetitive task.

But it is *not* true that tasks need to be codified to be automated. Modern machine learning techniques differ from classical AI techniques precisely on this dimension, as I explained in Chapter 2. If there are enough instances of the inputs that humans use to produce acceptable outputs, the underlying pattern can be extracted by the algorithms, even if the humans themselves were unable to articulate exactly how they achieve the results they do. That's the difference between teaching a kid how to ride a bike versus how to do long division.

Old rule-based AI could only learn the latter, and that's when the codifiability criterion made sense. Modern AI can learn both kinds of tasks. Tacit and non-codifiable expertise is no longer protection against automation using modern AI techniques if there is enough data. And for repetitive tasks, almost by definition, there will be a lot of data.

It is also *not* true that tasks must be simple for machines to be able to do well on them. One of the basic set of mathematical results about AI is that given a data set, there exists a deep learning algorithm that cannot be beaten in extracting complex patterns from that data.[89] Finding that algorithm through experimentation and research is of course not trivial, and for many problems we face today, the data we humans have from our life experiences far exceeds what can be made machine accessible. But the idea that there are complicated patterns in a dataset (accessible to both human and machine) that a human can see but a machine can *never* see, is false.

After November 2022, it became apparent, that it is also *not* true that creative tasks simply cannot be automated; that is precisely what the launch and widespread diffusion of GPT-3.5 by Open AI made clear. Creativity is defined as the generation of useful novelty, and anybody who has played with a generative AI tool like a chatbot or an image generator will find it hard to argue that these systems do not produce creative outputs. (Sometimes they are *too* creative: we call that 'hallucination'.) True, we don't know if they are creative using the same processes humans use, and their creativity is limited by their network architecture and training data. But our best guess today is that we humans, too, are limited by our cognitive architecture and our own life experiences.

Whether we are creative in the same way as machines or not, it is hard to argue that we retain a monopoly on creativity.

Put simply, advances in deep machine learning have already demonstrated that algorithms might have a relative advantage over humans even on tasks that are poorly codified, complex, and considered to involve creativity. This is more likely if these tasks exist in data-rich contexts, and involve, at their core, a prediction problem. Many tasks surprisingly turn out to do so (see Chapter 2). For instance, text and image generation are solved as prediction problems by generative AI. This implies that we should not blindly assume that it is only the low value-added and boring tasks we don't want to do anyway that machines can take over—we need a case-by-case analysis.

A second, and perhaps more profound, aspect to consider is the consequence of specialization, in the longer term, for human skills. Let's take a straightforward example. Suppose you must create a report summarizing recent sales data and forecasting future trends. Currently, you rely on tools like Excel, Word, and Tableau, as well as your own intelligence to crunch numbers and provide insights. Here are three possible scenarios:

- **Scenario A**

  Let's say you begin to use a machine learning algorithm that draws on a customer review dataset to do a language processing analysis. This improves the quality of your report. Much like before, the report essentially relies on your analysis with an added section.

- **Scenario B**

  Suppose you adopt an application that guides you in using your regular Excel data to fit a more sophisticated machine learning model with greater predictive accuracy. This effectively expands your capabilities. You're still very much the one doing the analysis and shaping the result, but AI tools expand your own skill set.

- **Scenario C**

  You no longer look at the data and simply rely on an algorithm to do the crunching and come up with an analysis of past trends as well as predictions about future sales. You then inspect the trends visually and offer your qualitative interpretation (as before). Overall, the algorithm is doing a portion of the work you did before.

What is the difference between these scenarios? While the quality of your final report improves in all three, your personal skills and capabilities remain unchanged (scenario A), increase (scenario B), or decline (scenario C). Should you really be indifferent in choosing between these three scenarios?

I could have easily replaced this example with others involving hiring, project investment, or supplier selection. But it's insight also applies to more micro-level tasks, such as creating a PowerPoint presentation, replying to emails, or drafting a business plan. In each case, you can use AI in ways that will maintain, enhance, or devalue your existing capabilities.

Think 'Outsourcing'

Corporate strategists will recognize the decision on how to use AI as very similar to those that companies face when outsourcing or partnering with others. Outsourcing relationships and strategic alliances between firms often feature collaboration based on specialization between parties whose interests are not fully aligned.[90] Each party may have a private interest in developing or learning skills the other party currently possesses, or to hold on to skills they currently possess to avoid dependence. One or more parties may even try to covertly learn the skills of the other through the relationship.

In essence, outsourcing involves reliance on external partners and potentially losing competence in outsourced tasks.

What competencies one chooses to give up through outsourcing has implications for resilience. We've seen the consequences of supply chains being globalized when the covid-19 pandemic hit us; in some countries, the skills needed to manufacture basic medical supplies had to be rebuilt from scratch at the very time they were urgently needed.

This does not mean one never outsources. Giving up on some capabilities by outsourcing them can be a deliberate choice made for strategic reasons, like to focus on developing other capabilities with the resources and attention released.

For example, a bank may decide that processing transactions or developing software is not core to its competitive advantages and choose to hive these tasks off to a vendor. Few of us lament the loss of navigational skills in the GPS era or manual laundry skills now that we have washing machines. We use that time for doing something else we value and, in a work context, that would mean developing new skills that we might have a competitive advantage at.

But companies also often adopt strategies that involve retaining certain in-house capabilities despite the economic case for outsourcing. For example, many automakers manufacture some volume of components in-house while outsourcing much of the rest.[91] Micro-processor chip manufacturers like Intel do R&D and file patents in technology domains that require chips, even if they're not themselves making direct sales in these domains.[92] This approach helps them maintain in-house skills as well as evaluate vendors and partners effectively. It also helps them wield bargaining power while ensuring supply chain resilience.

In sum, when corporate strategists consider outsourcing a part of their value chain to a vendor, they (ideally) do so with a lot of thought. They recognize that they are making a strategic decision on which competencies they are categorizing as non-core, which they would no longer invest in. They would certainly not give up something they consider to be core in the hope that technological progress will produce new activities for them to develop core competencies in. And even after they decide to outsource something, it would not be under the assumption that the gains from trade would be automatically and satisfactorily shared.

If individuals think like corporate strategists when 'collaborating' with AI, they will ask themselves the same kinds of questions. They would recognize that they are making a strategic decision on which competencies they are categorizing as non-core, and which they will very likely lose or never build, by relying on AI technologies. They would not give up something they consider to be core to themselves to AI, on the sheer hope that technological progress will produce new activities for them to become experts in. And even after they decide to rely on AI for something, it would not be under the assumption that the gains from trade would be automatically and satisfactorily shared.

Individuals may choose to hold on to skills or capabilities for reasons like resilience and bargaining power (as companies do), or preserving a sense of self-identity and efficacy. In such cases, one might prefer scenario B (boosting existing capability) over scenario A or C, even if the performance outcome (the quality of the report and/or the time taken to produce it) seems worse in the short term.

You should not be taken in by the language of 'augmentation' or 'human centricity' when applied to human–AI collaboration. These terms may conceal more than they reveal. For instance, all three scenarios plausibly fall under the augmentation category but the second is superior from the viewpoint of enhancing human skills. Human centricity can be an even more ambiguous label, unless backed up with the sort of precision we tried to develop in Chapter 3. Presumably, the better report you would produce in any of the above scenarios is good for at least some humans, namely your bosses! Labels such as augmentation and human centricity encompass a wide spectrum of impacts on your own capabilities, and it's up to you to safeguard them.

In many cases, it is not in the interests of employers to offload even entry level, low-end knowledge work to machines. This is because many (though not all) knowledge-intensive professions have a feature called a 'skill ladder' that my collaborator Nirmalya Kumar and I uncovered when studying offshore outsourcing of knowledge work.[93] Its existence in a particular career or profession implies that to do highly sophisticated, innovative work, a person must have engaged in less sophisticated work in the earlier stages of his or her career. Unless you climb the first rungs of the skill ladder, you can't get to the top. A person cannot become a partner in a consulting firm without having been an associate. Nor can an investment banker do so without serving as an analyst, a professor without having been a student, or the head of a clinical research team without having worked as a research assistant.

In each case, the junior people's contributions are valuable but often distinct from the work of senior people. Yet the senior staff members know exactly what their juniors do, because of the seniors' previous experience as juniors. Without such knowledge, the seniors arguably cannot do their own jobs effectively, which involve making use of input from juniors. One cannot skip steps on the skill ladder.

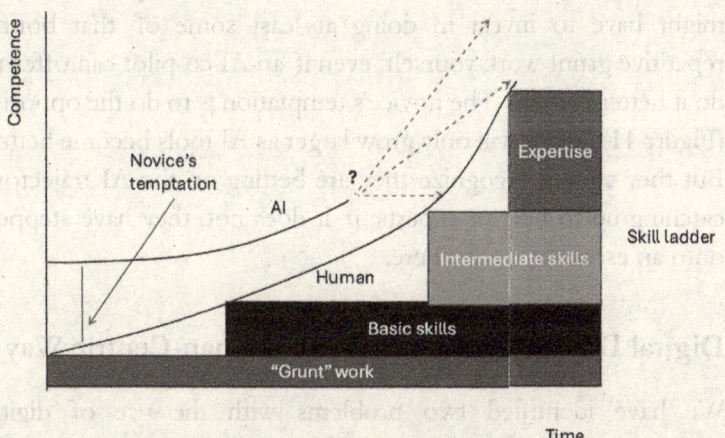

Figure 11: AI and the skill ladder

Organizations cannot get the steady supply of people for the higher rungs if the lower rungs of the skill ladder are effectively outsourced to machines. If they do, it is on the hope that the algorithms improve sufficiently to do the high-end work too, eventually (where the '?' occurs in Figure 11 shows three possible paths that AI competence might take). In fact, the act of beginning to automate the lower end of a skill ladder can be self-perpetuating. With the initial steps on the ladder removed, fewer people are likely to opt for careers that involve climbing the first few rungs. The limited availability of employees in turn reinforces automating the lower rungs of the skill ladder, and so on.

As these examples show, the decision to embrace AI and maintain or relinquish certain skills should be a strategic one, much like that we make when considering outsourcing and offshoring. Your choices should align with your goals and values, not by the appeal of ambiguous phrases like 'augmentation' or the seductive appeal of immediate convenience.

For organizations, the question to ask is how adopting algorithmic technologies will affect their skill pipelines (besides the effects on organizational context we have already discussed). For individuals, the existence of skill ladders implies that you might have to invest in doing at least some of that boring repetitive grunt work yourself, even if an AI co-pilot can offer to do it better for you. The novice's temptation is to do the opposite (Figure 11), and it will only grow larger as AI tools become better. But they should recognize they are betting on the AI trajectory catching up to human experts; if it does not, they have stepped onto an escalator to nowhere.

Digital Division of Labour: The Human-Centric Way

We have identified two problems with the use of digital algorithms in the division of labour. First, they might lead to hyper-specialization of the sort associated with digital Taylorism. Algorithms could chunk human work into such repeatable and boring tasks that work would become an intolerable drudge and eventually workers would be deskilled (and disempowered). Second, under the guise of relieving humans of drudgery, collaboration based on specialization between humans and AI algorithms could lead to humans being coaxed into giving up certain tasks and letting the associated skills atrophy. I have argued that the second is a more important problem than the first, but both need attention. Both are also related in the sense that specialization inevitably implies, among other things, de-skilling.

Are there ways in which we can use digital algorithms for division of labour that do not lead down these dark paths? I will point to two, though more are probably waiting to be discovered through a systematic search based on the logic of organizational context preferences (Figure 7).

Algorithm-Assisted Self-Selection

The process of breaking down objectives into tasks and matching workers with tasks—division of labour—has traditionally been a top-down exercise presided over by managers. However, it is increasingly recognized that organizational context preferences for autonomy, competence, novelty, and fairness can be met by letting the members of an organization self-select into the tasks they take on. Despite all the legitimate criticism about gig-work platforms, they do offer the ability to choose which tasks to take on, and gig-workers seem to value that.

In fact, at many software and consulting firms as well as less-hierarchical organizations like the video game producer Valve and auto-parts maker FAVI, self-selection into tasks has become the norm for its positive effects on intrinsic motivation, and for tapping into employee's own knowledge of what they are best at (something that managers may not easily be able to see). In some cases, the task division could still be done by managers, but workers then could self-select into tasks. In others, both task division and allocation can occur simultaneously through self-selection. For instance, in the case of open-source software development, the founders do not lay out a fully specified task structure as a menu from which subsequent entrants choose tasks. Instead, the very act of self-selecting what to do may specify the task division, just as the slices of a cake become defined as individuals cut themselves portions.

Yet there are some drawbacks to this human-centric approach in terms of goal centricity. In our research, my collaborators, Marlo Raveendran and Massimo Warglien, and I discovered that self-selection systematically produces a type of coordination failure: workers may not pay enough attention to the skills and preferences of other workers when they choose tasks.[94] Consequently, some tasks get over-staffed, and some remain under-staffed, and people may take on tasks that others are better qualified to do.

A non-human-centric approach would be to scrap self-selection, and instead let algorithms match people to tasks (perhaps even better than managers could). But there are algorithmic solutions that can preserve human centricity while also protecting goal centricity. In our research, we built computer simulations of many 'agents'—each a simple AI—which led us to discover two ways to make this happen.

First, we found that it helps to identify for what kinds of situations self-selection works well despite the tendency of people to ignore the skills and preferences of others. It turns out that when staffing for growth (i.e. all tasks are available, but workers become available at unforeseen times, as is typical in project-based organizations), when tasks can be performed independently of each other, and when each worker is uniquely skilled (specialized!) at some tasks that others are not, then self-selection does extremely well in terms of both goal and human centricity.

It's crucial to note that the specialization here is not imposed on workers but rather arises from the worker's own preferences and choices. The breadth of the tasks they are specialized in is determined by them, not dictated by managers.[95] Our findings imply that if you have many high-skilled workers who are specialists in different tasks, your organization will likely benefit from letting them choose the tasks they prefer (and we can use data to tell if your organization meets these conditions). The overall quality of work and motivation will be high, and there will be little risk of a less qualified worker 'blocking' a more qualified one from a task or leaving some tasks under- or over-staffed.

Second, algorithms can assist workers in self-selection by pointing them to tasks where they can make the biggest difference, not necessarily the tasks that they are personally the most skilled at (because somebody else might be even more skilled at that task). For instance, an algorithm can simply direct workers to choose among tasks that nobody is doing—much like ride-sharing apps direct drivers to rides that have not yet been picked up. But tasks can also be performed by multiple workers in knowledge work contexts like software development. Here, more subtly, algorithms may help direct workers to select from among tasks where they can make the biggest positive difference to the teams of workers who are already engaged on those tasks.

Skill-Preserving Collaboration Between Humans and Algorithms

As I have noted, at least some organization scientists are uneasy today about the rhetoric of augmentation (applied to modes of human-algorithm collaboration) acting as a cover for de-skilling and eventual automation.[96] The basic problem is that once humans specialize in some tasks and give up on others (that algorithms take over), this is usually irreversible. Many skills have a 'use it or lose it' flavour for the human, while the algorithm is likely to only get better over time at even the tasks humans currently do. I count the 'human as a gatekeeper' or 'human in the loop' configurations as also forms of specialization prone to the same risks. These involve humans exercising supervision or conducting final checks on work that has been given over to algorithms. But judging, evaluating, or overseeing something is not the same as being able to do the thing (try swapping the judges for the singers at your favourite Music Idol show and see).

An alternative that my collaborators—Vivek Choudhury, Arianna Marchetti, and Yash Shrestha—and I have been exploring borrows an idea from computer science called ensembling.[97] Contrary to the logic of specialization where humans and algorithms work on separate tasks, ensembling entails both doing the same task, either independently in parallel or in sequence/ iteratively. Why is this duplication ever useful? Because by combining their independently produced results, we can get an outcome that is superior to what either alone could have produced, if the errors of one can cancel the errors of the other.

Have you heard the story of the two statisticians who go out hunting, shoot, and miss their mark by the same amount in opposite directions, but claim they succeeded? Actually, they did, on average! Crucial to this story is that they are both off the mark in different but self-cancelling ways. This idea is very well known in social science as well. We have known that if each juror is at least marginally better than random chance at reaching the right verdict, the probability of a jury reaching the correct verdict increases with jury size. The average of a crowd's estimate (of anything—the weight of an ox, the temperature tomorrow) is more accurate than the estimate of the average person in the crowd.[98] These effects come about because even if the individual members of a group are all wrong, if they are diverse in the kinds of errors they make, their errors can usefully cancel out. It's crucially important to highlight that even the individual who is more wrong than the others can still contribute useful diversity in errors to the group.

A lot of knowledge work involves decisions, and all decisions under uncertainty ultimately require a prediction: What will occur if we do A versus B. For instance, when deciding which candidate to hire, or which project to invest in, we must predict what the outcomes would be if we selected each candidate or project. Using 'committees' of algorithms that make such predictions, each possibly making errors, but different errors that cancel out, is an old and now widely used trick in machine learning. That is where the name 'ensembling' comes from.

If you dig deeper into why the errors are different across the models used, why there is a diversity in errors, it turns out it comes from differences in the models used, differences in the data available to each model, and combinations of both differences. This is why we feel so optimistic about ensembling humans and algorithms. Our minds work differently from the way AI algorithms do, and we have access to very different kinds of data. This diversity in models and data could produce useful diversity in errors when ensembled. Crucially, collaborating in a model of ensembling preserves human skills, because we don't have to give up any sub-component of the tasks to algorithms. Further, even if humans underperform algorithms, we remain useful as contributors of diverse errors to the team.

Let's take an example. When hiring, HR personnel have to study CVs as well as interpret what they learned from interviews. A division of labour between humans and AI based on specialization could involve the humans focusing on interview data, and the machines reading CVs. In contrast, a division of labour based on ensembling might involve both humans and machines looking at both kinds of data and reaching their own decisions—to hire or not hire. We would then aggregate these decisions using some rule (e.g. hire only if both say yes, or a simple majority if there are more than two evaluators). The first approach with specialization runs the risk of de-skilling humans at reading CVs, but the second does not.

It's obvious why we should hesitate to use algorithms as oracles—they are not infallible even if they perform better than us. Our argument is that we should also think carefully before using them as assistants, since hiving off some tasks entirely to them can entail a loss of skills that we would in fact like to keep. The ensemble approach instead suggests using algorithms as colleagues—somebody who does something like you, who can offer a second opinion, whom you can learn from (since they do similar things), and ultimately, somebody who can be ignored!

Conclusion

Every organization has a division of labour, and specialization is not the only basis for it, despite its widespread use. High levels of specialization can produce efficiency. But it is not human-centric in a variety of ways: it can rob work of meaning and novelty and require centralized supervision that can impinge on autonomy. It can de-skill people in ways that are not to their advantage, or even to the organization's advantage.

Digital algorithms can accentuate the worst aspects of specialization, but again this is not the only possibility. Using algorithms to create divisions of labour that are mindful of OCPs can promote both human and goal centricity. I have outlined some ways in which this can be done, such as object-based division of labour and ensembling, but my examples are by no means exhaustive.

I can't stress enough that while the structure of OCPs is universal, which dimensions are valued most by a particular organization's members can vary enormously. Therein lies the importance of experimenting with alternative forms of division of labour involving algorithms to understand the impact on your own organization's context, and therefore for its human-centricity.

Chapter 6

Digital Integration of Effort

Imagine a time machine that can transport you 50,000 years into our past.

I picked this period for a reason. It's well before large-scale agriculture or cities, but also well after homo sapiens became a distinct species. Humans by this point in time would have become biologically the same as humans today—get them into jeans, T-shirts, and sneakers (and a shower first)—and you could pass them on the street without noticing anything amiss. They would have the same faculties for language, thought, and art, yet, they would have none of the technologies we take for granted today.

Let's say you step inside my machine and hit 'go': As someone intrigued by organizations and how they function, what should you expect to see?

The first thing that might surprise you is that while there are no corporations or governments in sight, you would undoubtedly observe organizations—groups of people working together to achieve goals. The best evidence we have today suggests that our prehistory was characterized by bands of humans, both kin and non-kin, living and working closely together to sustain and propagate themselves. These groups embraced what is known as a hunter-gatherer lifestyle—no settled cultivation, but rather a nomadic tendency to subsist off the land. There would be little by way of accumulated material wealth.

Like all organizations, these groups also faced the universal problems of organizing (Chapter 4). But their solutions differed vastly from what we are familiar with today. Hunter-gatherer groups are believed to have divided and allocated tasks (i.e. divided labour, the subject of Chapter 5) based on gender. They also integrated effort and handled exceptions quite differently from us.

First, these are small (~50 to 100) and their members are in near constant face-to-face communication. Everybody knows everybody. Membership is quite stable, with people living and working in these groups for decades, usually from birth. Second, decision-making and exception management handling within the group—where to go next, how to defend against attacks by other groups or resolve internal disputes—is surprisingly participative. There is unlikely to be more than one layer of hierarchy. We will see leaders, but not chains of reporting structures. Furthermore, these leaders will tend to be temporary, holding their position through prestige, and exercising their power through persuasion, not because they can intimidate the rest.

This picture of our pre-historic past is not based on speculation. Painstaking research over decades by anthropologists, archaeologists, biologists, and evolutionary psychologists have pieced it together, and it is now the dominant consensus among this community of researchers.[99]

Get back into the time machine and set the dial to jump forward—to about 5,000 years ago. Now you'd see the beginnings of the great civilizations around the world—in Mesopotamia, the Indus Valley, Egypt, and China. You'd see empires, and associated organizations with several thousands of members, in the form of religious orders, militaries, and state bureaucracies. A far cry from the hunter-gatherer groups of 50 to 100 people who knew each other since infancy, in direct physical contact with each other. Integration of effort and exception handling no longer relies only on direct communication, mutual adjustment, and consensus formation. Instead, we'd see hierarchies of authority and extensive systems of rules and procedures binding large groups of strangers together.

The ability to scale organizations well beyond the typical hunter-gatherer group was a remarkable human accomplishment. Trade networks, with goods exchanging hands across thousands of miles and diverse cultures are also impressive (you would see these too on this stop of the time machine), but I reserve my wonder for the miracle of getting thousands of strangers to collaborate on complex long-term projects without most of them ever having met each other.

Set your dial to 'today' and come back to now, where it is commonplace to see organizations with hundreds of thousands of employees. Some gigantic ones have millions (e.g. Walmart and Amazon, not to mention government bureaucracies in China, India, or the US). Getting such large groups of people, who are strangers to each other and who may never see each other physically, to collectively achieve goals, however imperfectly, is a staggering feat.

Perhaps an even more impressive fact: In all this time, the basic biology of our species (including how our brains work) does not seem to have altered much. But our cultural toolkit— the collection of ideas, beliefs, and hacks we have collectively put together through generation after generation of trial and error— has changed unrecognizably. Digital algorithms are only very recent additions to this bag of tricks.

What are the key innovations that have made it possible for us to organize on a large scale—in particular, how did we become so adept at integrating the efforts of large numbers of people, and managing exceptions and conflicts among them without the entire organization falling apart? And how will digital algorithms affect these capabilities? Will they substitute or complement the older ideas we have, and how will they affect the satisfaction of organizational context preferences and human centricity of organizations? These are the themes of this and the next chapter.

Large-Scale Organizing: Three Types of (Non-Digital) Innovations That Made It Possible

Our stop at 3000 BCE in the time machine showed us that we had figured out how to scale organizations far beyond the size of hunter-gatherer groups long before digital technologies made their appearance. How did we do it? I believe there have been three major types of innovations that have allowed this scaling.

To explain why I think so, I'd like to start with a simple question: What is the most basic constraint to scaling an organization? I believe it is **conflict**—everything ranging from subtle mistrust, through the breakdown in harmonious cooperation and coordination, all the way to violence—anything which makes it **difficult to reach agreement.** It's easy for small groups to organize themselves. They can often reach agreement through discussion and consensus on objectives and how to solve the UPOs—how to divide labour, integrate effort, and manage exceptions.

But this becomes tremendously harder once we get to larger groups, and there is a technical reason for this: if there are n people in a group, the number of potential dyadic interactions that can arise between them is $n(n-1)/2$. Why? Because everyone (n) interacts with everyone else $(n-1)$, and we divide by 2 to avoid double counting—me interacting with you is the same as you interacting with me.

Let's call the probability of any interaction turning into a conflict p, so that the expected conflicts in a group increase quadratically with n and linearly with p. Let's assume that beyond a certain number of realized conflicts, the group ceases to function effectively. The problem of scaling an organization involves increasing n without exploding conflicts beyond this level.[100] I'll stress again that by conflict, I mean all forms of disagreement— breakdowns in cooperation, misunderstandings, failure to converge—and not only acts of physical (or verbal) violence. I don't think the ideal amount of conflict is zero—we know that new ideas can come from the clash of perspectives. But there is a level of conflict above which the organization cannot function and may cease to exist.

Given how I described the potential for conflicts as depending on the number of interactions and the probability of each interaction turning into a conflict, two obvious strategies to reduce conflicts are to make each interaction less prone to conflict (i.e. reduce p) and somehow restructure the number of interactions for a given n to reduce their number (so that it is smaller than $n(n-1)/2$). I call these 'interaction smoothing' and 'interaction pruning', respectively. These contribute directly to integrating effort. But even after we apply these strategies, some conflicts might manifest anyway. We might need to create some capacity for managing these exceptions by 'absorbing conflicts', perhaps by resolving them, or finding some way to lower the impact on the organization of those conflicts.

These three basic types of solutions to conflict—smoothing and pruning interactions and absorbing the realized conflicts— give us a useful framework to think about the innovations that underlie our capacity to achieve integration of effort (through smoothing and pruning) and exception handling (by absorbing conflict) with ever larger numbers of people. It will also be useful to understand how digital technologies affect our capacity for organizing.

Let's consider smoothing first, which entails tuning down p. How can we lower the probability of an interaction between people becoming a conflict? We could align their interests through the right incentives. We could align their understanding and perspectives by making sure they can communicate well. Language, writing, and transmission (I'm thinking of carrier pigeons, smoke signals, and horse riders with messages here, nothing digital) all undoubtedly played a historical role. But in addition, an important discovery that allowed organizations to scale may have been the realization that shared cultural beliefs—norms, values, ideologies, even language—can do the work of smoothing. The examples we noted earlier of some of the earliest large-scale organizations such as religious orders, state bureaucracies, and militaries capitalized on shared belief systems.

Culture-shared values and beliefs can align what people care about, make it easier for them to communicate, and guide them towards reaching compromises when necessary. These cultural beliefs can come from a sense of collective belonging to a group, respect for a shared history, and an expectation of a shared future. If one can reliably socialize large groups of people into shared ideologies and beliefs, so much the better from the perspective of smoothing. This is why leaders care so much about creating shared visions, and why shaping the education of the young is such a powerful means of creating cohesive groups capable of large-scale collaboration. Even if the total number of interactions remained unchanged, i.e., it is still $n(n-1)/2$, through smoothing we have reduced the overall extent of possible conflicts.

Next let's consider pruning. One way to significantly prune the number of interactions for a group of fixed size is to restructure them into a 'group of groups'. This involves breaking down a large group of people into subgroups such that the subgroups can feature a lot of interaction within them but relatively little interaction between groups. This is also called modularization— we are chunking a complex system into modules with limited dependencies between them.

For instance, if you have a group of 6 people, then the possible interactions between them are 6*5/2 = 15. But suppose we create two subgroups of 3 people each: then within each group there are three interactions (3*2/2) and let's assume there's one interaction connecting the two groups. So, we have pruned the interactions from 15 down to 7 by breaking down groups into subgroups. And even if each interaction was as prone as before to turning into a conflict (i.e. no smoothing), you would still effectively have reduced the overall extent of possible conflicts. This dividing up social units into smaller subunits, which can work quasi-independently of each other and with relatively little need for interaction between them, turns a group into a group of groups. This is another type of innovation—again without recourse to any digital technology—which allows for large groups to still work coherently towards an overall objective.

Both culture and modularization have their limits as mechanisms to integrate effort. Smoothing via shared cultural beliefs, short of brainwashing, can't eliminate all conflicts. Creating sub-groups to achieve pruning assumes that we can break up the goals of the overall group to map onto the subgroups in a way that does not require much interaction between them, but the nature of work may make it impossible to avoid dependencies between groups. Both approaches also get harder to pull off at larger scales; maintaining shared culture in large groups is not easy,[101] and as the number of sub-groups increase, the interactions between them also increase rapidly.

Further, one strategy may hinder the other. For instance, interactions between subgroups become reliably rougher than those within them because of a process known as 'organizational differentiation'—sub-groups develop their own goals and internal culture and can treat other sub-groups with hostility.[102] Conversely, smoothing that reduces the friction in interactions can also make it hard to limit and focus interactions to subgroups.

That brings us to the third type of innovation—absorbing the conflicts that inevitably arise.[103] As groups scale and the possibility of conflict increases, it's useful to have an individual given the explicit responsibility of managing those conflicts, arbitrating them, and helping reach a final decision even when the group members can't easily agree among themselves. This is what the formal role of leaders with authority is primarily about.

'Authority' is the right to demand and receive compliance in a specified zone of action. It is enshrined in both legal and cultural norms. This was already present in an embryonic form in our ancestor's hunter-gatherer societies. But the crucial innovation lay in vastly scaling up the capacity of authority to absorb conflicts through delegation. How?

As any one single leader's capacity to absorb conflicts is limited, when a group increases in size, it becomes useful to have two sub-leaders now responsible for two subgroups, both reporting to an overall leader. This is feasible because the highest-level leader delegates authority to the sub-leaders to manage their respective groups. The process can repeat itself as the sub-groups grow larger. This is how chains of authority produce many-layered hierarchies and allow us to create larger and larger organizations.

Note that this is not the same as pruning interactions by creating 'groups of groups', where the subgroup need not have any leaders (or any overall leader). Rather, hierarchies of authority combine the creation of sub-groups with a branching chain of bosses. The latter adds significant capacity to absorb conflict, making it possible to scale-up to a far greater degree than what could be accomplished by forming subgroups alone.

Modern organizations today continue to rely heavily on these three innovations. CEOs are obsessed with creating shared cultures to smooth interactions, the organization chart crystallizes (in varying degrees of detail) the group and sub-group structure that allows for pruning interactions, as well as the reporting relationships that capture the hierarchy of authority that is meant to absorb conflict. None of these solutions are infallible of course; cultures may be weak or fragmented in practice, the grouping structure might ignore the reality of interdependence between groups, and the chain of command may be more like a leaky garden hose than a fibre-optic cable when it comes to transmitting authority and information. But they have nonetheless brought us a long way from the hunter-gatherer groups we encountered 50,000 years ago.

What's next? How will digital technologies, including AI algorithms, change how we prune and smoothen interactions and how we absorb conflict? How will these technologies affect how we build cultures, create subgroups, and deploy hierarchies of authority? Will the new solutions be human-centric? Hierarchies are important enough to deserve their own chapter (the next one). For the rest of this one, I will focus on answering these questions for pruning and smoothing interactions—the innovations that help integrate effort at scale.

Digital Pruning and Smoothing

Today, digital technologies profoundly shape how we organize to achieve goals. In fact, most interactions in most organizations of any reasonable size are already mediated or shaped by some kind of digital technology—email, text chat, video conferencing, etc. But the covid-19 pandemic that led to large-scale shutdowns of offices and initiated mandatory working from home forced reliance on digital technologies for organizing to levels that were unheard of. This has also generated some interesting innovations in how we organize ourselves.

I want to focus on five types of innovations that differ from each other significantly. They are by no means the only digital technologies that matter for integration of effort, but I focus on these for two reasons. First, I have studied them. Second, I think they illustrate the range of possible ways technology can impact integration of effort: if we were to place these on a line, at one end would lie technologies that help prune interactions, and at the other end lie those that help smoothen interactions (Figure 12). And somewhere in the middle are those that do a bit of both.

Smart coordination rules	The "git" approach	Interaction in Virtual reality	Thought translators	Culture constructors

"Pruning" interactions				"Smoothing" interactions

Figure 12: How algorithmic technologies can aid integration of effort

Algorithms as 'Smart Coordination Rules'

Pruning interactions to contain conflict requires reducing the number of interactions between n people to a number lower than $n(n-1)/2$. As I have noted, we have been doing this with non-digital technologies for a long time, by creating sub-groups. But another, perhaps more recent, approach involves using coordinating rules of various kinds—schedules, standards, and interfaces. If each person follows the rules, they will be automatically aligned, without needing to interact directly with each other.

For instance, traffic rules aim to make interactions between drivers very simple. If people abide by the rules, there is no need for active interaction or trust in each other. But formulating the rules is not a trivial task even in a relatively simple system (e.g. traffic) with few and well-understood interdependencies that involve getting people to move without banging into each other.

In general, to understand how to prune the interactions in a system requires a deep understanding of the underlying task structure and the ability to craft appropriate metrics, information flows, and incentives so that interactions between people can be fully embedded in the rules themselves. But the nature of interdependencies in many contexts are neither few, stable nor well understood, making it very difficult to formulate useful coordination rules to prune interactions. Rules that are incomplete, and worse, inflexible may sometimes be worse than no rules. The rigidity of bureaucracies and the rules they are made up of is legendary.

Making the rules digital—in the form of software programs— helps solve some problems. Specifically, the rules can be made far more complex. Some believe that this is also how distributed ledger (blockchain) technologies and smart contracts can help to scale collaboration among large numbers of people with limited interaction among them. I am less optimistic, because most current smart contracts are not that smart; critically their capacity to adapt based on data is limited. In fact, their main claim to fame is their immutability (i.e. they cannot be changed) and automatic execution with limited human intervention once certain conditions are met.[104]

To see this clearly, let's consider two situations. First, imagine a set of vendors who are part of your supply chain and need to provide raw materials of specific quality for specific prices. In this scenario, smart contracts can work effectively because the requirements and conditions are well-defined and quantifiable. Smart contracts can handle the quality parameters for the raw materials, the prices for different types and quantities of raw materials. The smart contract can be programmed to release payments or trigger other actions based on specific delivery conditions, such as delivery dates, locations, or verification of received materials. The transactions and executions of the smart contract can be recorded as a permanent, immutable record (e.g. a blockchain), providing transparency and an auditable trail for all parties involved. The reason smart contracts can work well in this example is that the requirements and conditions are objective, quantifiable, and can be clearly defined upfront.

Now consider another set of vendors: third-party engineers, marketers, and graphic artists who have to help you come up with a new design for sports apparel. In this scenario, smart contracts may not be as effective because the requirements and conditions are subjective and prone to change. Design elements, aesthetics, and creative concepts are highly subjective and difficult to quantify or encode. The design process is often iterative, with multiple rounds of feedback, revisions, and changes based on stakeholder input and market trends. In this case, making the rules of interaction digital via smart contracts does not really help. Smart contracts thrive on clearly defined rules and conditions that can be objectively verified and executed. However, in the case of a creative design process, the requirements are heavily reliant on human judgement, creativity, and collaboration.

In sum, the nature of interactions must be very well understood to be able to convert them into rules, since the rules are not capable of developing that understanding for themselves. That's why smart contracts are still largely restricted to settings where interactions are simple—in the sense all parameters and outcomes are fully specifiable up front. Such situations may be the exception in the larger scheme of things.[105]

This is where the next generation of digital technologies—based on AI—can play an important role by acting as 'smart coordination rules'. Rules embedded in AI algorithms can be both far more complex and can also evolve over time based on data (see Chapter 2). If people align to the algorithm, they become aligned with each other, without needing to interact with each other (and thereby avoiding the possibility of conflicts). Imagine a traffic system that is embodied as an app that sits on your smart phone, which tells you which lane to take and what speeds to drive at. If all drivers used the app, traffic could be routed to make maximum use of the roads (even reversing traffic flow directions frequently) while keeping everyone safe.

Digital platforms that employ gig workers embody this approach, but it is not restricted to pruning the relatively simple interactions that such platforms currently rely on when transacting online, food delivery, or ride-sharing. The world of software development offers a useful alternative preview of what the 'smart coordination rules' approach to pruning interactions can do, even when applied to complex, innovative, and creative work.

Coders have been using continuous integration (CI) tools for a long time to work on different portions of a software program without having to actively worry about their changes creating problems for other coders. The technologies take care of that behind-the-scenes coordination. Each time a coder adds to a program, CI tools automatically check for compatibility and whether the code runs.

It is the equivalent of an editor reading all submissions to a magazine as they come in to make sure they fit well together into a coherent issue, that there is no overlap or redundancy or flat-out contradiction. CI tools represent the automation of the coordination work that would otherwise have been conducted by humans. Researchers who have studied the use of these technologies have found that they free up coders from (what they consider to be) tedious coordination work, enabling them to focus more on their individual contributions.[106]

In some ways, where coders lead, other knowledge workers seem to follow, a little later. The sort of embedded automated coordination that coders have been using for a decade or more has diffused widely among knowledge workers through applications like Google Docs during the pandemic. Features like version control, a hierarchy of editing rights, and automatic saving has taken away the bother of keeping track of who is working on the most recent version, and how to make sure that others don't make changes that disrupt your work.

To get closer to CI for knowledge work, think of genAI applications that can take texts written by different authors, each a specialist (possibly even in different languages) and integrate them to produce a single, integrated document. Providing real-time suggestions to the authors as they each work independently (possibly without even giving much thought to the other's existence), the algorithm can effectively prune the interactions between people. This is already technically feasible. We can imagine the same sort of approach to ensure legal and regulatory compliance of all the proposals for new activities a company performs, or of integrating healthcare data collected at various points in a patient's journey through a medical system.

Will this algorithmic pruning of interactions lead to human-centric organizational contexts? It is easy to see the negative effects on human connection. For instance, early data from the use of Microsoft's Copilot genAI technologies suggests that users lower the time they spend in meetings—they can rely on an AI to summarize the discussion for them instead.[107] While this can indeed free up valuable time and improve productivity, it also means less time spent in social interactions. Losing these sources of social capital is not great from a goal-centric perspective either, since the interactions produce the connections that people leverage to ideate and pursue opportunities. The competencies of individuals might also become narrower, as the give and take of coordinating with others broadens our own thinking.[108] Gig workers are already known to be struggling from the lack of social connection that characterizes their highly modularized and individualized work (that is algorithmically coordinated).[109]

But recall that organizational context preferences (see Chapter 3) are multidimensional. Besides connection (relatedness), people also value autonomy, competence, fairness, purpose, and novelty in their organizational contexts. People also weigh these differently. Recall also that the software developers who use continuous integration algorithms report feeling empowered to focus more on individual contribution and less on coordination. So, we should note the dangers posed by pruning interactions to gig-worker levels, but it is useful to bear in mind that for individuals who place less weight on social connection, there may be compensating effects on other dimensions. As always, the question is how to match organizational contexts to people with specific OCPs.

Almost Telepathy? The Git Approach

Next, we turn to an approach that incorporates both pruning and smoothing of interactions. Typically, when people work on complex tasks, the default is to work face-to-face. This offers the virtues of 'synchronicity' and 'media richness'. By this I mean that the time lag in the interaction between two or more individuals is almost zero when they are co-located, and working face-to-face conveys soft social and background contextual cues (it's still hard to sense other people's reactions in a group Zoom meeting). When the pandemic began in 2020, I think it is accurate to say that no technologies existed that could near-perfectly replicate these two properties of social interaction among physically proximate people. The result was an explosion in video calls—the closest, imperfect substitute we had through platforms like Zoom, Teams, and Skype.

But there is an alternative approach to collaboration using digital tools that explicitly avoids trying to replicate 'in real life' (IRL) interactions. It was also pioneered in the software development industry and entails asynchronous interaction— with people working in parallel and contributing at different times to a piece of software without directly talking to each other. It is in some sense the exact opposite of face-to-face work—it is neither synchronous nor involves many social cues. It sounds like a recipe for chaos, but it is not.

Open-source software development in particular could not function unless it worked in this asynchronous way because it has voluntary contributors around the world contributing what they can, when they can. At the heart of this approach is the 'git' workflow process for software development, invented by Linux founder Linus Torvalds. In this process, a programmer contributing to a body of code 'forks' (copies) the code, so that it is not blocked to other users (who can continue working on it in parallel), works on it, and then makes a 'merge request' to have the edited version replace the original. The accepted new version becomes available for other contributions.

The process separates responsibilities between those who accept merge requests ('code maintainers') and those who make them (contributors). Further, contributors must rapidly submit a minimum viable product (MVP) to avoid redundancies produced by people working on the same thing in parallel. Shared folders and version control systems (that we have now all become use to through technologies like Dropbox and Google Docs) help keep everybody's work coordinated.

While this way of working was mainstream in the world of open-source coding, it wasn't very common outside that world before the pandemic. That's why my collaborator Marco Minervini and I became interested in a startup called GitLab well before the pandemic began. GitLab developed tools that allowed software engineers to slice a complex project into chunks, work in parallel on specialized tasks, then put the pieces back together again into a functioning whole. Apart from its extraordinarily rapid growth, we thought GitLab was noteworthy for at least three other reasons.[110]

First, like many technology companies, it used its own tools—GitLab (the company) used GitLab (the product) to make improvements in GitLab (the product). Second, even more unusually, it also used the same set of tools to organize and manage itself, not just write code. For example, the company handbook, which exhaustively documented its formal organizational structure and processes, was itself developed, maintained, and edited as if it were a code repository. Anybody could 'fork' a copy, make changes, and then submit a 'merge request' that a designated senior manager could then decide whether to approve. It's hard to keep me away from anything *that* meta!

Third, it was one of the largest 'all remote' commercial organizations in the world. From its founding in 2014, GitLab had maintained an all-remote staff that exceeded 2,000 employees spread across over sixty-five countries by 2024 (they went public in 2021). No two employees at GitLab worked long term physically in the same place.

Yet, this extreme distribution of work did not translate into an avalanche of emails or Zoom calls. Instead, GitLab leaned heavily on parallel, asynchronous working as embodied in the git process, even for non-coding-related knowledge work. For instance, a senior leader might announce a new proposal for a strategic initiative, request asynchronous feedback from across the company within a fixed time window, and then schedule a single synchronous video call to agree on a final version of the initiative.

This is the 'git' approach: separate responsibilities between maintainers and contributors and encourage contributors to quickly submit MVPs. MVPs are a means to cope with the fact that pruning cannot be perfect—work cannot be modularized completely. Instead, you force each interdependent party—who is working independently—to take the smallest, feasible yet reversible, step, observe the impact on overall system, and revise. This prevents the efforts of one person from damaging or duplicating those of others.

GitLab also insisted on its employees using chat and bulletin board platforms like Slack, not email. Employees posted all questions and shared information on the Slack channels of their teams (later the team leaders decide what information needs to be permanently visible to others). This was because parallel asynchronous work can easily be mis-coordinated unless the people doing it have a fair amount of shared knowledge and understanding of what others are up to. This is what digital collaboration tools inspired by the 'git' approach essentially do. They reduce the need for face-to-face conversation or even video calls by creating a stock of easily visible information about what others have already done, are doing in real time, and plan to do next, while allowing parallel work on the same documents.[111]

In a study of offshoring of innovation work more than a decade ago, I had noted that to a naïve observer, the extent to which people can coordinate their work in this way without the need for direct communication may seem almost like telepathy.[112] Today, many of the tools that support the git workflow have percolated out of coding into the world of knowledge work in general.[113] Like Google Docs, these tools enable parallel work and version control, mutual observability of work tasks, a hierarchy of editing rights, and automated execution. They are found useful even by people collaborating while sitting in the same office, not just thousands of miles away.

This approach to smoothing interactions (lowering p, the probability that interactions turn into conflicts) using digital technologies essentially gives up on replicating IRL interaction. The founders of GitLab were aware that asynchronous remote working of the kind they relied on could not supply much in the way of social interaction. They recognized it as a weakness, because social interaction is not only a source of pleasure and motivation for most (think of the Organizational Context Preference for connection and relatedness; see Figure 7), but it is also where the 'random encounters', the serendipitous exchanges by the coffee machines and lift lobbies, create opportunities for ideas and information to flow and recombine. In some sense, during the lockdown, we were drawing down on the stock of social capital we had built up through face-to-face interaction, but it has got to be replenished somehow.

GitLab tried to make up for the lack of social interaction in a few ways. Each day, teams were encouraged to hold optional social calls, staggered to be inclusive of time zones. These had no work-related agenda—they were just an occasion for informal contact. There were Slack channels dedicated to helping people with similar non-work-related interests (cats, dogs, music, gardening, etc.) connect to each other. And once a year, the company tried to bring everyone physically together at a retreat.

But as one of the founders noted to us, in the end GitLab was going to attract people who simply did not set as much weight on social interaction (at least at work) as most did. That is, by definition, not a large set of people, but if it is big enough for GitLab to access, their model can be viable.

AR/VR: *The Matrix* . . . or *Teletubbies*?

And now for something completely different (as the Pythons would say)—in fact the exact opposite of the GitLab approach.

Do you remember *Second Life*? It was (briefly) big in the early 2000s and involved a digital platform where users could together do versions of real-life activities in a shared virtual world. I was an enthusiastic early adopter, and (briefly) thought that my limited social skills IRL could be more than compensated by my charismatic avatar (who, for reasons I cannot fully explain, looked rather like Idris Elba). After realizing that much of the time my digital self was merely walking around jerkily among other equally wooden-looking digital characters, I exited the platform. Though I did not know the term then, this was a 'rage quit', because the platform was nothing like the 'metaverse' I wanted it to be. The metaverse was a term coined by sci-fi author Neal

Stephenson in a novel that described an exciting vision of virtual interaction that was hard to tell apart from IRL stuff. And the novel had come out a decade earlier.

Inspired by the growth of distributed working in the pandemic, Meta (formerly Facebook) decided in 2021 to make a public commitment to developing the metaverse. Today the term has come to refer to a technology platform that allows for immersive social interaction across a variety of virtual spaces, mediated by avatars (digital representations of users). The immersion is aided by virtual reality (VR) headsets (currently still clunky), that give users the subjective experience of being in spaces they can explore, move in, and communicate in together; the images could be projected onto the real world creating augmented reality (AR). Most of the early use cases lie in gaming and music. Several performers have already held concerts and fashion houses have auctioned digital replicas of their products on metaverse platforms for real money.

Can the metaverse and augmented/virtual reality technologies enable a form of smoothing by improving collaboration in the workplace? Unlike git-inspired digital collaboration tools, the metaverse explicitly aims to recreate many if not all of the properties of IRL interactions, particularly synchronicity and media richness. True, interaction sessions for now on most metaverse platforms look more like an episode of *Teletubbies* than the sort of seamless virtual reality that could spell the death of distance. But when my collaborator Vivianna Fang He and I took stock of the developments recently,[114] we came away optimistic that these technologies will become an important form of interaction smoothing, for three reasons.

First, more realistic seeming avatars are coming, rapidly. Technologies that can fool your senses into thinking you are in the same room as a distantly located collaborator already exist.[115] Second, many of today's video gamers—no less than a sixth of the global population, by some estimates—will become tomorrow's employees, and they may not even mind the cartoonish avatars as much.[116] If you are unfamiliar with how gamers in their teens (and beyond) interact socially in multiplayer online games, then you are missing out on a very important source of insight into what social dynamics in the metaverse might look like. How gamers bond, form and break relationships, collaborate and compete may be indicative of how they will interact in a virtual work environment in the future.

Third, and perhaps most importantly, mentally simulating interactions with imagined and remembered others is nothing new for us as a species. We are hardwired to seek relatedness and connection, true. It is also true that for a significant portion of our evolutionary history, that connection occurred face-to-face in small groups. However, when human societies scaled in the form of tribes, communities, and nations, we have been able to maintain connections not only with people who are present, but also with those who are either remembered or imagined. VR technologies represent another iteration on this idea.

We are still early in the stages of understanding how VR-based social interaction can affect the satisfaction of organizational context preferences such as relatedness, novelty, and fairness of work contexts (by masking demographic markers that are often the basis for discrimination, for instance). The data on social interactions gathered via metaverse platforms suggest both exciting opportunities for understanding better how homo sapiens collaborate, but also dark possibilities for manipulation and deception. Avatars can camouflage ill-intentioned actors, and even be a front for AI algorithms trained to exploit you. The European Union's AI Act explicitly forbids companies from deceiving individuals into thinking they are dealing with humans when they are in fact dealing with an AI. Emerging social contracts and regulation will no doubt shape human-centric use

of these technologies, which allow distributed and remotely
located individuals to interact smoothly.

Algorithms as Thought Translators

Effective communication is essential to integration of effort,
and we are already very familiar with digital technologies that
can enable it by connecting people at a distance and also by
translating between languages. However, conveying meaning
can be challenging even to speakers of the same language. My
collaborator Özgecan Koçak and I have been fascinated for a
long time with why words do not always convey meaning reliably.

The core issue is that different groups of people working
on different problems develop their own jargon. This produces
'fuzziness' in language: the same words can come to mean
different things across the groups, and they might use different
words to mean the same thing. Consider the words 'attrition'
and 'turnover' in business contexts—depending on whether you
sit in marketing, HR, or finance, these words probably mean
different things. Surprisingly, the first problem (i.e. the same word
meaning different things) is harder to solve than the second (i.e.
using different words to mean the same thing), because it requires
unlearning the associations between words and their meanings
for one or both parties. Communication between them becomes
correspondingly difficult.[117]

If disagreements arise, the challenges of communication can
also make it hard to understand the root cause of the disagreement.
We can disagree on what we think is true, or what we think is
desirable.[118] Imagine a discussion in a boardroom about whether
the company should adopt a new clean technology that will lower
emissions further below the legal limit. The company is already
compliant with regulations, and disagreements can stem either
from scepticism about whether the new technology works as

claimed, or whether it is valuable to lower emissions further to keep the environment clean, at a cost to the shareholders. But the fuzziness of human language can make it hard to tell which of the two is driving disagreement.

It turns out decoding what we are saying to each other, particularly when we are disagreeing, is hard. We might understand the words coming out of each other's mouths but still fail to mutually understand the thoughts we are thinking. Can digital algorithms help to smoothen our interactions by doing this decoding for us?

I noted in Chapter 2 that generative AI technologies like ChatGPT can work as 'general purpose translators' mapping between any two sequences—of words, pixels, genes. They can of course do this at scale (e.g. in an online conversation involving dozens or hundreds of people) and at great speed. Our initial studies show promise that they can also be trained to parse the sources of disagreements between people into those arising from beliefs about what is true versus what is considered desirable.

We think it is possible to build 'AI mediators' that can, in real time, smoothen our conversations. They can detect misunderstandings, note unremarked points of agreement, diagnose true sources of disagreement, and feed this back to us. This could improve the quality of our discussions and make it easier for us to collaborate. Risks to data privacy will have to be considered, of course, but do not seem any more daunting than our current use of transcription features on Zoom. From the perspective of organizational context preferences, AI mediators seem like relatively benign technologies.

Constructing Culture

The last application of digital technologies I discuss is a subtle one that also acts through smoothing, though the technology is completely behind the scenes, the interactions remain human-to-human.

Widely shared cultural beliefs—values, norms, and assumptions—play an important role in producing alignment and smoothing interactions between the members of an organization. Conversely, failures of collaboration, such as those observed after mergers and acquisitions or in the aftermath of too-rapid expansion through hiring, are often attributed to cultural factors. But how does one construct a culture?

Broadly speaking, there are only two ways to build cultures that we know of. The first involves socialization, which is changing the cultural beliefs that people hold through a process of persuasion, either top down from the leaders of the organization or peer-to-peer from colleagues. Socialization requires interaction, communication, and opportunities for learning from feedback, and not merely the grand gestures or speeches by the CEO.

The second approach to building a culture involves *sorting*. This occurs at the hiring or selection stage, as well as at the retention stage where managers can encourage people with ill-fitting beliefs to depart (while keeping those who fit well). Though I have no definitive evidence on the matter, I strongly suspect that sorting is typically more powerful than socialization, as the latter requires un-learning.

Digital technologies can intervene in both socialization and sorting. We have already discussed online interaction, and it is easy to imagine the role of metaverse applications in building teams and onboarding new employees. Here, I will focus on sorting.

Algorithm-assisted hiring, where information from CVs and the transcripts from interviews are used to make hiring recommendations, are a reality. Text analysis algorithms can be trained to automatically filter applicants based on, say, words (institution names, college degrees, etc.) on their CVs.[119] Algorithmic hiring can amplify sorting based on cultural attributes, and thus help create strong cultural alignment.

There are at least two types of risks to human centricity here to consider. First, algorithmic hiring can be biased. In one infamous example, Amazon[120] had to stop using machine learning for hiring because the algorithm made gender-biased hiring recommendations. Today we understand that the bias in such situations may lie in the social process the algorithm is being trained to emulate, even if the data and the algorithm themselves are unbiased. If an organization systematically does not promote or hire candidates from an ethnic or gender minority, then models trained on data from the past hiring and promotion practices will likely perpetuate this bias.

Sophisticated users of machine learning have developed a suite of measures to check for fairness in predictive analytics, and this should become an integral part of any applications that use people data. One possibly surprising solution is **random selection**—for instance if some fraction of hiring occurs at random, this would allow for an unbiased training set for the algorithm.[121]

A second problem is that digital algorithms might be so good at sorting that they produce culturally homogenous cults with little diversity of thought (even if there is superficial demographic diversity). If we believe that algorithms using data can detect cultural alignment better than humans, by matching organizational contexts to the preferences of people for instance, they might magnify the worst aspects of cliques. This is already visible in the polarization and echo chambers we see today on social media, which are the algorithmically boosted results of existing human tendencies towards parochialism and groupthink.

In principle, this problem also has algorithmic solutions. We could instruct algorithms to connect or hire a fraction at random or for difference in cultural values and opinions. One can break the walls of echo chambers through the algorithmic insertion of diversity. But it is a problem we must think proactively about if we continue down the path of algorithm supported hiring and socialization.

Conclusion

The covid-19 pandemic was a major transition point in digital collaboration for organizations around the world. Businesses realized their real estate costs could drop as the percentage of onsite employees decreased. There was also a possible sustainability bonus. In the United Kingdom, for example, 25 per cent of transportation-related emissions are attributed to the daily commute, and transportation is the sector with the largest carbon footprint in many economies.[122] In many ways, covid-19 may have turned out to be 'the great decongestant'—pushing back against the forces of agglomeration economies that also end up producing crowded and polluted cities.

Yet, none of this depended on the invention of new digital technologies for collaboration. In the first half of 2020, as organizations the world over scrambled to adapt to working remotely, it was not because of any immediate new breakthroughs in digital technologies for collaboration. Rather, necessity created by lockdowns led to a surge in adoption of existing tools, from Slack and Microsoft Teams to Trello and Asana, and human ingenuity took off in improving on how to use those tools to prune and smooth interactions. We adapted.

But since then, we have had new technological breakthroughs. Some like VR/AR and the metaverse still are far from mainstream, others like generative AI have had more immediate success. There can be little doubt that these will shape the nature of distributed work and collaboration going forward.

In this chapter, I have described five types of digital algorithm-enabled innovations that affect our capacity for integration of effort. The list is not exhaustive. Rather, it illustrates a spectrum of approaches ranging from pure pruning of interactions to pure smoothing. Developments like these innovations also pose a different set of challenges than what the pandemic did, when we had to adjust to the rapid onset of clearly undesirable circumstances. Unlike the pandemic, technological innovation is ongoing; the central concern is guarding against the unintended, undesirable consequence of adopting what seems desirable.

This is why it is so crucial to ask how every new digital collaboration technology satisfies the organizational context preferences (Figure 7) of its users. The structure of these preferences has deep roots in our evolutionary history as well as more proximate roots in our cultural conditioning,[123] and cannot be assumed away if we want to make human-centric choices about which technologies to adopt.

If anything is clear about the future of work after the pandemic, it is that 'all remote' and 'all in the office' are unlikely to be the optimal design for any but a small fraction of organizations. Rather, some measure of distributed work will likely be the default arrangement, with who comes in to work and how often becoming an organization design choice to be made differently in different contexts. Digital algorithms for integration of effort will be in the foundations of these arrangements. Let's lay them in carefully.

Chapter 7

Digital (Non)Hierarchy

Supervising prisoners of the state is hard work. They are unlikely to be the most peaceful and law-abiding folks around (that's probably why they are prisoners). They get into dangerous fights, with each other and with the supervisors, and they try to escape. In the UK, it is common to see one supervisor for every three to five prisoners.[124] Incarcerating one hundred prisoners might thus take thirty to forty supervisory officers arranged into a hierarchy of as many as five levels—from Officer to Prison Governor (they can be identified by the number of stripes on their epaulettes).

Could you possibly do away with all this hierarchy? Have just a handful of supervisors managing large numbers of prisoners? In 1787, two brothers, Jeremy and Samuel, conceived of a way this could be done. Jeremy Bentham is more famous as the founder of utilitarianism—a philosophy that suggests that we seek to obtain the 'greatest happiness of the greatest number' of people.[125] But I want to focus here on his ideas for prison reform, and one innovation in particular, that he (along with his brother, Samuel) proposed, which could lower the burden of supervision on prison officers.

Their idea worked like this: Imagine a large compound in which the prisoners were free to move about, with a circular tower in the middle. A single officer in the tower could oversee everyone because the tower was circular. Of course they could not oversee everyone at once. But they did not have to, because the prisoners could not observe who the supervisor was observing—it was a tall tower and the proposal suggested using blinds.

This was the Bentham brothers' brilliance. If no prisoner could be sure whether he was being observed, it would be better for all prisoners to behave properly. Presto, one supervisor, dozens of prisoners! Since it's hard to prune or smooth interactions (see Chapter 6) to avoid conflicts among the prisoners, this solution instead scales up the capacity of a central actor to observe and deal with conflict.[126]

Jeremey Bentham had several visionary humanist ideals that have become mainstream today, and the brothers conceived of their design as a humane alternative to the prisons of their day, which rarely allowed prisoners out of their cells. They also argued that the good behaviour of the supervisors would be guaranteed by the fact that they in turn would be observed by the public.

Much to the Benthams' chagrin, this design, called the *panopticon* (derived from the Greek term for 'all seeing') was never built. Nonetheless, the panopticon has entered popular discourse as a metaphor for coercive control of the many by the few via observation that is itself hard to observe. For instance, Shoshana Zuboff has effectively employed the metaphor to describe how managers might observe employees through stealth monitoring technologies by detecting keystrokes or log-in times, and how technology companies like Google and Meta may covertly observe, but also covertly shape customer's behaviour through their technologies.[127]

The point I wish to make here is somewhat different though. The panopticon was a social technology, based on a physical design that allowed a supervisory hierarchy to be replaced by one or a handful of supervisors. If you want to 'flatten hierarchies'— get rid of layers of management—it is not going to get more dramatic than this. But I doubt even the Bentham brothers would have argued their design had produced greater empowerment for the prisoners. The panopticon vividly illustrates that **flattening a hierarchy does not automatically imply either decentralization or empowerment**.

Multilayered hierarchies with high degrees of centralization generally do poorly on many of the dimensions of organizational context preferences (OCPs) (See Figure 7). The effects on suppressing autonomy are obvious. Closely related are perceptions of unfair differences in benefits and status between levels. In multilayered systems, roles inevitably become more narrowly defined and specialized when descending the ladder. Further, those at the upper layers often impose standardization of processes and procedures for creating alignment overall. Consequently, curiosity, variety, and versatility may all get short shrift.

If we care about increasing the human centricity of organizations, we might want to use digital technologies to build, not the panopticon, but the collaboratory.[128] A term coined by the computer scientist William Wulf, the collaboratory describes a digitally enabled system for peer-to-peer collaboration without centralization or hierarchy.[129] Instead, individuals organize themselves into groups as the need arises using digital tools for sharing information, collaboration, and tracking progress. When it works effectively, there is little need for supervision. It is also 'flat', but unlike the panopticon, its flatness is likely to be accompanied by greater decentralization in a manner that enhances many aspects of OCPs.

Hierarchy and Centralization

Let's first get the tricky relationship between centralization and hierarchy straight and dispel some myths about both.

Centralization refers to inequality in the extent to which the members of a group can affect the group's behaviour. If everybody can influence the group's behaviour and outcomes equally—through discussion and a vote for instance—we can say the group is fully decentralized. If all decisions for the group are made by one person (e.g. a team leader), we say the group is fully centralized.

A hierarchy (of authority) refers to a multilayered structure, with those in higher layers exerting authority on those below. Typically, we would require at least three layers (e.g. a CEO, manager, and worker) to talk about a hierarchy.[130] Hierarchy is correlated with centralization but is not the same thing. A hierarchy is necessarily more centralized than a completely 'flat', perfectly decentralized group, because the person at the top can influence a group's behaviour more than the others.

But two organizations with the same number of layers in their hierarchy could differ in the extent of their centralization, based on how much authority is delegated. In fact, it is possible that a four-layered hierarchy is more decentralized than a three-layered one, if there is a lot of delegation of authority in the former relative to the latter. After all, we could have very high centralization even in a flat two-layered group, like the panopticon. It's a myth (and a mistake) to equate the layers of hierarchy and the extent of centralization in a system, even if they are correlated.

Another myth to bust is that decentralization necessarily implies greater autonomy and that it will always be valued positively by employees; that decentralization equals empowerment. Unless accompanied by modularization that allows for independent action, decentralized decision-making forces people dependent on each other to reach agreement and coordinate; and in such situations, strong forms of social control by peers instead of by superiors may arise.[131] From being controlled by a boss, we may transition to being controlled by our peers.

Further, OCPs matter but so do material rewards. In organizational contexts, autonomy is freedom from behavioural control, but it is usually accompanied with greater accountability for outcomes. When a subordinate is granted autonomy on how to perform a task, they are still (and perhaps more) likely to be held accountable for outcomes. Therefore, for risk-averse individuals, an increase in autonomy, unless compensated with more pay, may leave them worse off since they also bear more risk.

Finally, while autonomy is part of the OCPs, it is not the only dimension, and decentralization may increase autonomy while hurting other aspects such as fairness. High autonomy systems place the burden of what managers used to do on employees, and some may see this as exploitation. For instance, in self-managed teams, the tasks of scheduling, coordination, and conflict resolution now fall to the team members, which in a hierarchical team would have been the responsibility of a manager. That's more work, which is not always compensated. Therefore, we should think about decentralization as a possible means to increase the satisfaction of OCPs but not as guaranteed to do so.

But isn't hierarchy hardwired into our nature?

No, you are thinking of our evolutionary cousins, chimpanzees and gorillas. These primates do indeed have hierarchies of dominance, with those at any layer lording it over all those in the layers below. But the overwhelming evidence is that homo habilis, our ancestors, diverged from primates about 2.5 million years ago, and homo sapiens (us) branched off and lived in flat, decentralized systems from about 200,000 years ago to about 13,000 years ago.

Humans, through a combination of social skills (to form coalitions) and weapon use (which equalizes differences in physical strength) seem to have figured out how to tame the most dominant individuals in their groups.[132] As a consequence, human groups became in general less centralized and less hierarchical than those of our primate cousins. Instead, two-layered structures (leaders and followers) with a high degree of decentralization seems to have been the norm.

My collaborators, Jayanth Narayanan and Mark Van Vugt, and I examined the literature on the matter carefully and concluded that if there is anything genetic in our disposition towards how we want to be organized, it is in the direction of minimizing the dominance of powerful individuals in groups, not happily settling into a layer where we accept being bullied by all above in return for being able to bully all those below.[133] The pecking order we see in modern corporations is closer to chimp (or even chicken) than human in spirit. It does not reflect an innate preference for centralization but may rather reflect constraints that frustrate a preference for decentralization.

This conclusion is consistent with the best syntheses we have today of modern human social psychology as it manifests in organizational settings—as found for instance in Edward Deci and Richard Ryan's Self-Determination Theory (which we have encountered in Chapter 3 when we first described organizational context preferences).[134] These authors have analysed a vast amount of evidence to conclude that the need for autonomy is a fundamental human motivator (i.e. the freedom from domination by others). Since centralized control necessarily implies a reduction in autonomy, this suggests a widely held preference for avoiding being at the base of a centralized, hierarchical system. This innate antipathy to centralization may be one reason why even dictators persist with the pretence of holding elections.

It's worth highlighting that one may dislike being at the receiving end of authority in a centralized, hierarchical system but have no qualms about (or even like) being able to exercise it over others. For years, I have been entertaining my students and myself by first offering them a choice between jobs in these two companies (see Figure 13a)—the jobs are identical in job title, job description, salary, and work conditions. Only the org charts and where the jobs are located are different. Overwhelmingly, the majority choose the one on the left because it is 'less hierarchical'—there are fewer layers between them and the CEO.

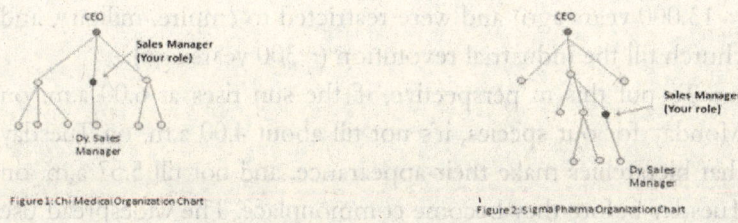

Figure 1: Chi Medical Organization Chart   Figure 2: Sigma Pharma Organization Chart

Figure 13a: Which job will you take?

But then I offer them the next pair of choices (Figure 13 b), again with identical job title, job description, salary, and work conditions. The majority now choose the one on the left because they have a layer below them.

Figure 1: Alphexon Medical Organization Chart   Figure 2: Omega Pharma Organization Chart

Figure 13b: Which job will you take now?

In other words, when my students say they 'don't like hierarchy', what they really mean is they don't like hierarchy *above* them (i.e. have many people with power over them). They have no problems with the hierarchy below them (i.e. having authority over others).

True, it's difficult to find organizations of any meaningful size today that do not have a multilayered hierarchy. Yet, this is by no means guaranteed to remain so in perpetuity, nor has it been eternally so. On the larger timescale of two hundred thousand years of existence of homo sapiens as a separate species, multilayered hierarchies of authority are recent cultural artifacts. To the best of our knowledge, such structures either did not exist at all or were rare before the agricultural revolution

(~13,000 years ago) and were restricted to empire, military, and church till the industrial revolution (~300 years ago).

To put this in perspective, if the sun rises at 6.00 a.m. on Monday for our species, it's not till about 4.00 a.m. on Tuesday that hierarchies make their appearance, and not till 5.57 a.m. on Tuesday before they become commonplace. The widespread use of multilayered hierarchies of authority is no older than a few moments in our history. It is not a fact of human existence to be taken as much for granted as being born with a belly button.

This digression into our remote past allows us to dismantle yet another myth. The preference for decentralized organizing is not merely a Gen Z (and beyond) effect or the 'next stage of human consciousness'.[135] Rather it is very likely to be universally valued, though to varying extents. My own analysis of data from the World Values Survey (see Chapter 3) also supports this view. Economic prosperity may make the articulation of this preference louder, and the need for autonomy seems to be increasing over time, not over generations. Independent of whether flat or non-hierarchical organization designs like 'holocracy', 'teal', or 'humanocracy' are fads, the desire for more decentralized organizing is not a fad.

In fact, given how recent they are in our organizational landscape, multilayered centralized hierarchies may be better described as the fad!

So why do we have multilayered hierarchies?

If, as I have argued, hierarchy and centralization are not 'natural' to our species, why do we find ourselves living and working in organizations that are centralized hierarchies? If it's not a hardwired preference for hierarchy, what is it? An important part of the answer, I believe, comes down to two limits: the limit to scaling consensus, and the limit to scaling centralized control.

If a group of people could consensually agree (through discussion, voting, or any combination of these) on how to organize themselves to achieve a goal, there would be no need for centralized decision-making by a manager. Peer-to-peer discussion and agreement would suffice, as when friends get together to organize a party.[136] But consensus becomes harder to achieve as groups get larger. Managers become essential when groups can no longer manage themselves.

As we saw in the previous chapter, the possibility of conflicts and disagreements in an organization increases non-linearly with scale. Two possible approaches to controlling conflicts we discussed there in depth were to 'prune' and 'smooth' the interactions. For instance, through control of sorting into and out of the system and socialization, and by modifying the properties of interactions among the actors, it is possible to reduce the possibility that unresolved conflicts accumulate. However, neither approach is infallible, nor always possible.

The third approach, as I noted in Chapter 6, is to 'absorb' conflicts, and centralization is a powerful absorber of conflicts. Authority—the legitimate ability of A to demand compliance from B in a particular domain of action—creates centralization in a group when only one or a few have it. By centralizing decision-making authority in the hands of a single individual, we create capacity in the system for a dedicated conflict resolver.

This is why large parties and events benefit from event managers who can make final decisions and put a stop to endless discussion, and who specialize in overseeing execution, whereas small events may not. Consensus is also harder to achieve as the members in the group become more different from each other in terms of their expertise, background, and interests. If the party is going to be organized by a group of strangers, a manager of sorts will be necessary. Finally, consensus is also harder to achieve as the dependencies between individuals become complex and need to be negotiated. A themed party will need a managerial role to help align and execute decisions about food, music, décor, and costume.

Put simply, organizing based on peer-to-peer consensus is easier when groups are small, similar, and simple. As groups get larger, more heterogenous, and the dependencies between people become more complex, consensus-based organizing breaks down. Enter centralization, in the guise of a manager. By centralizing the group, they help achieve coherence to the group's actions.

But managers are human too (Dilbert's arguments to the contrary notwithstanding). There are limits to how many individuals a manager can effectively supervise. As the group of subordinates that they oversee grows larger, more diverse in their skills, backgrounds, and interests and the work they do grows more complicated, the burden of supervision will grow till it maxes out the managers supervisory capacity. This is the limit on the manager's span of control.

To overcome this limitation of centralized control by one manager, what do we usually do? We divide up the original group into two sub-groups and assign each of them their own middle-manager, both reporting now to the single manager we started with (see Figure 14). And that's how we get a multilayered hierarchy.

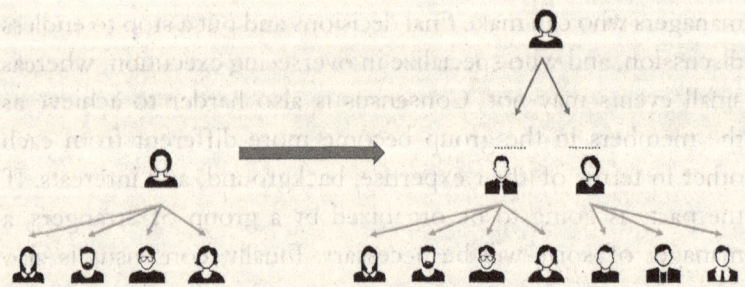

Figure 14: How hierarchies add layers

Can we keep doing this forever, and keep scaling up? No, because it gets harder and harder for the managers at the top to effectively impose centralization on the system. Information and control 'leak away' across multiple layers of managers. Instructions get garbled, and oversight becomes ineffective.[137] This is still the limit to scaling centralized control. It shapes both the maximum size an organization can attain while still functioning effectively, as well as the number of layers in the hierarchy of authority.[138]

To summarize, hierarchies with varying degrees of centralization are prevalent today because of limits to scaling consensus and limits to scaling centralized control. As we have gone from living in hunter-gatherer societies to today's societies, the organizations we live in are typically no longer small, they involve tasks and dependencies between them that are no longer simple, and they are made up of individuals who are often strangers to each other and no longer similar to each other. Consequently, we have found centralized hierarchies a useful means of absorbing conflicts, when attempts at pruning and smoothing do not suffice. It is the same old story we encountered first in Chapter 5: scale, specialization, and centralization reinforcing each other (see Figure 10).

However, besides the negative effects in terms of human centricity, centralization and hierarchy also have costs from a goal-centric perspective because multiple layers impose delays and distortions in the flow of information. In fact, much of the rhetoric of corporate flattening is primarily about the benefits in terms of speedy decision-making, and references to 'empowerment' are likely to be disingenuous, for reasons we will see below.

Centralization is an attempt to refashion a collection of many minds in the image of a single mind, and for our species, multiple minds beat a single mind at solving most types of problems. So even from the purely goal-centric perspective of increasing our collective problem-solving capacity, if we could find effective ways to organize while dialling back on centralization and hierarchy, we should. And we have tried to do so.

Experiments in Decentralized and Non-Hierarchical Organizing

How successful have attempts at doing this been? In my view, only partially.

Recent and well-researched books on flattening and delayering hierarchies have looked closely at widely publicized examples of profit-seeking entities that seem to operate in a decentralized and non-hierarchical manner, and I've been trying to understand the intricacies of how they work for over a decade through my own work. Prominent examples include companies like the US-based video game developer Valve, Dutch nursing services provider Buurtzog, French auto-parts maker FAVI, as well as the entire class of online entities such as decentralized autonomous organizations (DAOs). These have been written about extensively, so I will not repeat a description of them here.[139] It suffices to say all are famous for having no or very few middle managers, instead having individual contributor roles with considerable autonomy.

On closer inspection, some of these turn out to be flat but quite centralized, sometimes with single individuals (often the founders) exercising enormous influence (even if they do so subtly). One is left wondering about the robustness of these organizations to the eventual, inevitable departure of the founders from the scene. Others, like many DAOs, have adopted the trappings of decentralization with no managers and voting-based decisions. But look closer and all votes are not equal; they are weighed by economic stakes. The result is closer to shareholder democracy with the plutocrats in control, which I submit is not a shining example of decentralization.

Yet others have consciously chosen to keep their organizations small, similar, and simple, to minimize the need for centralization and hierarchy. Some take a bonsai approach, choosing not to grow—it is easier to be decentralized when small. Some adopt smoothing strategies by carefully sorting employees based on cultural fit and focusing on those who strongly value OCP dimensions like autonomy over other dimensions, even relative to pay. Some prune interactions by modularizing work or simply ignoring dependencies where possible.

These decisions are not without adverse consequences for goal centricity, such as limiting profitable expansion by staying small, curtailing innovation from diversity, and giving up on coordinating for economies of scope and synergy across groups, in order to give each group significant autonomy. To compensate, they generate a motivational bonus from fulfilling OCPs (particularly those related to autonomy and fairness). But most profit-maximizing companies seem to find this point on the trade-off unfavourable, which is why the high-profile examples remain curiosities and are not mainstream. The current 'market share' of these non-hierarchical forms is small relative to the 'mind share' they occupy in the rhetoric of modern management practices.

I think there is no real mystery any more to how any of the widely publicized instances of decentralized and non-hierarchical organizing 'do it' today. But after we have understood how they do it, it's not clear we can learn much that can be directly applicable to other contexts.

Indirectly, however, studying these strange inhabitants of the 'organizational zoo'[140] has shown us the underlying structure of the problem with great clarity:

1. If we want to organize at scale *without centralization*, we must find ways to break the limits on scaling consensus. This means we will need to find ways to improve how groups, even large ones, can manage themselves through consensus and collaboration.

2. If we want to organize at scale *without hierarchy*, we must
    find ways to break the limits on scaling consensus or on
    scaling centralized control. The latter will entail finding
    ways to expand the capacity for supervision by managers,
    and thus their spans of control.

Flattening an authority hierarchy thus requires increasing
managerial capacity to supervise or reducing the burdens of
supervision placed on those managers by their subordinates by
allowing them to collaborate more effectively. Put differently,
'flattening' hierarchies by removing layers without increasing the
capacity for collaboration and/or supervision is likely to fall flat!

Reshaping Hierarchies Digitally: The Good Way (and the Bad)

To keep organizations human-centric, I believe we should
prioritize the development of digital technologies that allow us
to break the limits to consensus, not the limits to centralized
control. We should aim to make individuals and groups capable
of managing themselves, not increase managerial capacities for
supervision. Why?

My reasoning is simple: making managers more capable of
supervision will flatten the hierarchy because each manager will
have greater spans of control. This will improve goal centricity,
but it may not improve the human centricity of the organization,
since the degree of centralization need not decrease (it may
even increase). However, if we make individual members more
competent at organizing themselves consensually, then there will
be less need for centralization, and therefore also fewer layers
of managerial hierarchy. This can improve both goal and human
centricity of the organization.

By this reasoning, the digital collaboration technologies we
discussed in detail in the previous chapter—algorithms as smart

coordination rules, the 'git'-inspired approaches to knowledge management, AR/VR, AI mediators and algorithmic hiring, and team formation—are all examples of potentially 'good' uses of digital technologies to dismantle hierarchies. My collaborators, Piyush Gulati and Arianna Marchetti, and I have found in our work that when companies adopt such digital collaboration technologies, they increase their advertising for new hires with job descriptions that emphasize the capacity to work without managerial supervision (indicating greater decentralization), and simultaneously reduce the ratio of managers to employees in the company (indicating less hierarchy).[141]

Let's consider the 'bad'. The term 'algorithmic management' has come to refer to the use of digital algorithms that (help) do what managers did. To understand how digital algorithms may change what managers do, it is useful to first consider what managers do at a more granular level. The research suggests that there are five basic functions managers perform for the groups they lead:[142]

1. **Supervision:** Managers motivate, monitor, mentor, and coordinate group members and act as dispute resolvers, i.e., exception management in the universal problems of organizing (UPO) framework.

2. **Representation:** Managers act as ambassadors for the group.

3. **Resource allocation:** Managers decide how to allocate scarce resources across competing claims within the group, as well as invest on behalf of the group by selecting from among competing alternatives.

4. **(Re)design:** Managers decide how the group must divide labour and integrate efforts (i.e. task division, task allocation, reward distribution, and information provision in the UPO framework).

5. **Entrepreneurship:** Managers also look for new opportunities for the group.

The higher in the hierarchy a manager is, the more likely they perform all the five functions including those closer to the bottom of the list. In other words, managers at all levels of the hierarchy will have some supervision responsibilities, but only those at the top may also undertake redesign and entrepreneurial functions.

Algorithms, particularly those based on generative AI, are now able to assist even with redesign and entrepreneurial functions, though there is some way to go before we can rely entirely on them for these functions without human supervision. Talk of 'AI CEOs' is as of today more gimmick than game changer.

But when it comes to supervision, which is core to the managerial role at all layers in a hierarchy, we already have a fully developed set of algorithmic tools. These can be used today to monitor, evaluate, and reward workers. These supervision technologies have the potential to tighten the control by managers of their subordinates because of the comprehensive amounts of data collected. At the same time, the rapidity and opacity of the algorithmic actions leave limited scope for preventive or corrective actions by humans to avoid harm.[143] A recent survey of over 170 articles on algorithmic management found that most documented the enhanced control of subordinates by supervisors, as in gig-work platforms like Uber.[144] These are flat but monitoring intensive, digital equivalents of the panopticon, and seem well deserving of the label of 'Digital Taylorism'.

In sum, algorithmic management can enhance managerial capacities at their tasks, and so they effectively expand managerial spans of control. Hierarchies can become flatter, but centralization does not decrease (or even increases). There may be gains in goal centricity but not necessarily in human centricity.

The Collaboratory versus the Panopticon

Many minds can do much more than a single mind. But they must first agree on what to do and how to do it! This is the problem that centralization solves in human organizations—to produce convergence and alignment despite the different things that multiple minds know and want. But centralization has its limits; it reduces the quality of the group's thinking to that of the individual who has sole authority. And when expressed through multilayered hierarchy, it can lead to delays and decoupling between knowledge and decisions.

These challenges to goal centricity could find remedies in digital technologies that amplify centralization. However, centralization can also lead to uncomfortable power differences and even outright exploitation. Turbo-charging centralization with digital technologies will not help with this challenge to human centricity. It might just leave us at the mercy of the panopticon—without many layers of hierarchy but with an extraordinary concentration of power at the apex.

This is why I think it may be more fruitful to think about the opposite approach: how to make decentralization more effective using digital technologies. The word 'heterarchy' refers to a system in which the sub-units have no stable ranking over each other; it is a group of groups that may be constantly evolving in their relative importance as the overall group adapts to changing circumstances.[145] **My arguments imply that we may be better off building digital heterarchies rather than digitally reinforcing traditional hierarchies.**

We have identified the challenges to decentralized consensual organizing that arise as groups cease being small, simple, and similar. Scale and specialization, as I have argued, stimulate centralization in a mutually reinforcing dynamic (Figure 10). Perhaps it will be useful to fashion digital technologies to attack these root factors that contribute to the limits of decentralization and throw us into the clutches of centralization. In other words, we might give priority to thinking about digital technologies that make the collaboratory more effective. I see at least three directions to pursue.

First, algorithms can reduce the scale of human organizations. Automation can directly lead to smaller organizations (or at least organizations with fewer humans in them). Smaller groups can find it easier to manage themselves than larger groups. As a corollary, if automation removes precisely those repetitive tasks from human hands that they find most tedious, this can help meet competence and curiosity-related OCPs. But this is, of course, a mixed blessing—it's not clear if reducing the number of humans in the organization should count as progress towards human centricity!

Perhaps in a more benign manner, algorithms can be used to prune interactions to convert large groups into smaller subgroups. This requires decomposing the overall group's goals into sub-goals that can be tackled by the sub-groups. This is algorithm-assisted division of labour, which we encountered in Chapter 5. This allocation need not be at the level of micro-tasks as in gig work platforms like Amazon Mechanical Turk or Upwork. Rather, clusters of interdependent tasks, loosely coupled to others, could be identified for sub-groups to work on relatively independently. For instance, Slack and Microsoft Teams facilitate this by allowing teams to create channels or groups focused on specific projects or tasks, enhancing decentralized collaboration and reducing the need for hierarchical oversight.

Second, algorithms acting as smart coordination rules that perform continuous integration of human knowledge work (Chapter 6) could make interactions within and between groups simpler and less prone to conflict. Till recently, algorithms were no match for humans at resolving unstructured and unstable coordination problems; this is what managers did well, hearing all sides, smoothing over conflict, and delivering final decisions that could be seen as legitimate. But the genAI revolution suggests we might soon have AI agents capable of managing behind-the-scenes coordination between human actors, possibly in ways that the humans do not even notice. For example, Zoom and Google Meet can integrate with AI-driven scheduling and coordination tools that automatically manage meeting logistics and follow-ups, thereby reducing managerial burdens.

Third, algorithms can be used to compose (sub) groups based on similarity of values while preserving demographic and intellectual diversity (i.e. increasing similarity within groups on some important dimensions, while preserving diversity along others). Humans organizing themselves in decentralized systems often display tendencies like in-group favouritism, groupthink, homophily, and cliquishness. Algorithmic sorting could avoid this. For instance, platforms like Upwork use algorithms to match freelancers with projects, based on a combination of skill sets and client needs, but one can imagine building in criteria to ensure both diversity and compatibility. Such harmonious grouping of employees can create effective norms for lateral dispute resolution, which are critical for self-management.

Crucially, algorithmic technologies might allow us to repeat these processes of (sub) group-formation as frequently as needed, possibly at lower costs than what we currently face with major reorganizations. For example, Asana and Trello enable dynamic project management where teams can be reconfigured quickly in response to changing project needs, supported by algorithmic task allocation and progress tracking. AI technologies can improve the sorting and matching needed to form new teams rapidly and effectively, acting as coordinators and mediators as I described in the previous chapter.

Conclusion

Throughout this chapter, I have highlighted the differences between building the collaboratory and the panopticon. Digital technologies that improve collaboration help with the former, whereas 'algorithmic management', at least as currently practiced in the form of hyper-monitoring, do more of the latter. What we build is our choice. I have made my own preference clear but let me add one last argument that might cement yours too.

I have nothing to say about the scientific and technical aspects of the existential risk we confront from climate change since I am not an expert on these matters. However, as an organization scientist, I can observe that the problem cuts across the boundaries of nations, and therefore requires different national governments to be able to collaborate and reach convergence on how to act (the same is true of AI regulation or data protection). Treating each nation as a distinct member of a global organization, reaching convergence among these 195 members, who differ significantly from each other in interests and perceptions is bound to be difficult. Of course, nations are not individuals, but they are represented by individuals. A meeting among the partners of a law firm or a consultancy, where each partner leads an organization of their own, is a useful reference point.

There is also one fundamental difference. The mechanism of absorbing conflict through a higher-level authority, which is potentially available to all other human groups (including law firms and consulting companies, via a managing partner) is not available to this group; there is no pan-global government in existence or in the offing. This means that this global organization has to reach order and avoid climate disaster without centralization. Almost paradoxically, failure to tackle climate change can result in resource scarcity and disorder within nations, pushing them to become internally *more* centralized and hierarchical, supporting a rise in authoritarian regimes.

If we want to avoid this, we simply have no choice but to improve our capabilities for the remaining two means of scaling consensus without authority that I have discussed: pruning and smoothing interactions between nations. That need not only entail better ways to obtain multilateral cooperation among all 195 at the same time but could also include ways of creating and supporting multiple islands of cooperation—the age-old 'group of groups' trick we have encountered before in Chapter 6 in our discussion of pruning interactions.

While there is no formal global hierarchy that can impose order on all nation states, sub-groups of nation states can be orchestrated by influential central actors, as in the political coalitions surrounding the US and China today.[146] We might also need a mobilized citizenry who can pressure their nation's representatives to strike the appropriate compromises and reach agreements with their counterparts, as well as implement those they do manage to agree on. And we will almost certainly benefit from multiple approaches and mechanisms at the global scale, just as organization designers pay simultaneous attention to modularizing work, building culture and influence through the leadership hierarchy, as they try to manage large-scale collaboration. It is unlikely there will be a single solution.

In other words, we have no choice but to build a global scale collaboratory, and no choice either but to experiment with how to do it. Figuring out how to organize at scale without centralization or hierarchy is, in a very real sense, *the* 'Manhattan project' for today's organization scientists. Experiments and trials at the organizational level, using digital algorithms to prune and smooth interactions, may help us in that project.

PART III

A WAY FORWARD

Chapter 8

Democratizing Organization Design

The capacity to organize may be humanity's most significant and oldest accomplishment. But our lives today are also influenced by another, more recent, human achievement: digital algorithms. Throughout this book, we have grappled with how to balance human and goal centricity as organizations adapt to digital algorithms.

There are, no doubt, many ways in which we can bring together the central ideas developed in this book, such as the recursive application of the universal problems of organizing at different levels in an organization, testing for the impact of organizational changes on organizational context preferences, and the importance of data-driven design. A lot of my excitement and enthusiasm as a professional organization designer comes from wanting to see all the interesting ways that our field will come up with to combine ideas like this into useful frameworks for action. But I'd like to end this book by outlining a vision for a new approach to the practice of organization design that I think can be particularly effective in bringing these ideas together—'decentralized designing' (DD).

The ideas behind DD germinated a decade ago in conversations with my long-time collaborators, Oliver Alexy and Markus Reitzig. This approach builds on three key ideas (Figure

15): first, an organization's design can vary across different
sub-units in an organization down to the level of small groups
(rather than one-size-fits-all approaches); second, those designs
should emerge through local participation in the design process
(rather than be dictated top down); and third, how useful these
designs are should be assessed, before adoption, through data and
algorithms (rather than based on opinions alone). I believe DD
offers a powerful integration of ideas that can help balance goal
centricity and human centricity of our organizations.

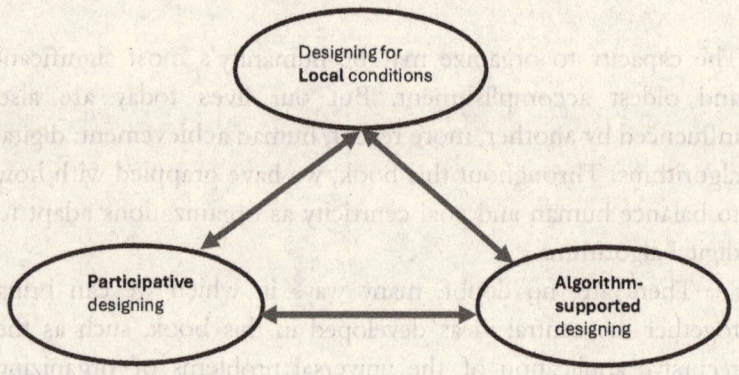

Figure 15: The pillars of decentralized designing

Note that DD is *not* the same as a decentralized design. Rather, it
is a decentralized designing process, where members of distinct
units of an organization can locally and participatively design
their own units using data that they are comfortable using. The
resulting design may well centralize a lot of decision-making to a
local leader and acknowledge accountability to a global source of
authority.

We already have many useful frameworks to do organization
design such as Jay Galbraith's Star Model, Peters and Waterman's
7S Framework, and Nadler and Tushman's Congruence Model that
are mindful of the twin objectives of goal and human centricity.[147]

Why do we need another? Put simply, we need it because of the recent explosion in the availability of organizational data, what (intelligent) algorithms can now do with it, and the prospects and perils they imply.

The DD approach, I argue, makes it much more likely that the double filter of goal and human centricity is rigorously applied to any new design change proposal, whether in the context of adopting new technologies or otherwise. Further, it is an approach that is very compatible with the use of advanced data analytics and genAI technologies as tools to assist in organization design in an ethical and human-centric manner.

Before we look at DD in detail, let me sketch out what it might look like in action. Let's imagine a mid-sized courier company with distribution centres—each with fifteen to twenty employees—across the United States called fast parcel services (FPS). Let's say FPS implemented a DD approach within a framework of common design principles. All centres would adhere to core values of safety, reliability, and customer satisfaction, and follow standardized processes for package handling and tracking. They might also share a common technological infrastructure and compensation system.

Within this overarching framework, FPS could allow each distribution centre to design its own organizational structures and processes to best achieve these common goals. In Atlanta, for instance, the centre manager might implement a flat, agile self-managing team structure, that takes an employee-led approach to solving the universal problems of organizing (UPOs) (Figure 8). This is because she believes it would empower her young, tech-savvy workforce to innovate within the established processes. The Chicago centre might opt for a more traditional hierarchical team with a manager-led approach to solving the UPOs to leverage the experience of its veteran staff in maintaining consistent quality.

To reach their respective design choices, each centre engages its employees in the design process, always keeping the overarching common principles in focus. In Atlanta, the centre manager might organize hackathon-style events where employees propose organizational models that could enhance safety and reliability. In Chicago, they use digital collaboration tools to run an iterative design process, ensuring all proposals align with FPS's core values and technological infrastructure. Crucially, all centres make a data-based decision on the design they choose. They run simulations and do pilots to check if the designs they are proposing can work.

Let's look at DD in detail keeping this example in mind.

Balancing Global and Local Design

The first pillar of decentralized designing involves striking a balance between global (organization wide) and local (sub-unit level) designing.

There will always be some common elements of design for all the units in an organization. These might be instituted to ensure accountability, transparent financial reporting, and to ensure compliance with the law. They may be necessary because the units are technically interdependent in a way that requires some degree of centralized coordination (e.g. common supply chains, shared IT infrastructure as in the FPS example, or integrated product development). These design choices at the global level can have enormous consequences for the entire organization, as all its units will inherit these choices and must deal with local consequences.[148]

Therefore, it is a good idea to make decisions that have global implications for the organization only when strictly necessary and make them with the highest standards of evidence possible. randomized control trials (RCTs) (see Chapter 4) can be useful here, and it is feasible precisely because of the large number of independent units (or independent clusters of internally interdependent units) that must potentially adopt these global design choices. Individual units, however, may still need to 'fill in' the rest of their detailed design choices—how to do task division, task allocation, reward distribution, etc. These units may be too small to conduct randomized trials. They will necessarily have to rely on experiential learning—learning through their own trials and errors and from those of other units in the system.

I can hardly claim this 'diversity in designs' by itself is a new idea. It is quite well documented, for instance, that there is considerable diversity in designs within multinational corporations as each country unit adapts to local conditions. Franchise chains are also known to be quite explicit in stipulating global design principles and at the same time allowing for local flexibility in choices appropriate to local markets. I am merely arguing for taking it down to the smallest organizational units that have identifiable, distinct goals, namely groups, teams, and committees. Why? **Because these have become the new smallest units of organization design (OD), given the data we now have.**

To see this, it's useful to contrast decentralized designing with other popular OD frameworks such as the Star, 7S, or Congruence models as well as the classic menu of designs such as divisional, functional, transnational, and matrix structures. A strength of these macro-design frameworks is that they encourage a holistic view of the organization (as in they look at the entire macro-structure of the company, and not its parts). But holism of this form has its limits. Organizations, particularly larger ones, have become so enormously complex (think about reporting to multiple bosses, working across locations, the need for integration with external partners, and participation in ecosystems) that attempts to design an entire organization or even large chunks of it in a holistic way are simply not as useful anymore.

These limitations have become increasingly visible over the last few decades through the need for frequent reorganizations. None fixed old problems completely, and all created new ones, which in turn needed reorganization again, and so on. The only people left smiling were the lucky consultants who made money each time. An important reason for this 'repetitive reorg syndrome' is that designs are often standardized to the level of the entire organization. This is what organization-wide macro designs, such as functional, divisional, product, regional, and matrix, do.

A divisional structure, for instance, assumes that throughout the organization, it will be true that collaboration between functions pertaining to the same product line is more important than within functions, and that this is uniformly true for all functions and product lines. This assumption of global uniformity keeps things (from the CEO's perspective) simple and elegant but may do more harm than good. Where it is inaccurate, the design creates problems that once they become visible enough, trigger another reorganization. Decentralized designing in contrast allows for differentiation in design. Every team within a corporation is an organization that could have a different design, subject to a broader common framework. Large-scale reorganizations should become less frequently necessary.

The macro-design frameworks like the Star Model, the 7S Framework, and the Congruence Model were formulated well before the Big Data revolution. In the absence of better data, these frameworks were very useful for senior managers to form a useful if highly imprecise picture of all the interactions that needed to occur in an organization and make high-level decisions that could perhaps influence them in useful ways. The primary lever at a senior manager's disposal was the organizational chart (and its implied reporting, incentives, work interdependence, and information flows), even though all the macro-design frameworks emphasized that hiring and socialization practices were also important.

But today we have data at the level of individuals, and their interactions with each other in the teams they work in as well as between teams. Continuing to depend solely on high-level constructs to deal with OD would be like using telescopes to design micro-chips; they are just too crude as instruments. In contrast, the DD approach operates at the level where the data resides—individuals, teams, and networks. It provides the conceptual microscopes we need.

The DD approach can unleash a 'superpower' of a system comprising many smaller, nested, and loosely coupled units—it's evolvability. This insight also came from Herbert Simon, who laid out the logic in a landmark paper.[149] Complex systems, by definition, involve lots of linkages between their components. But the pattern in which those linkages are arranged matters for the vulnerability of this system to changes in its environment. When the sub-units of a system are arranged in a nested and loosely coupled way (i.e. with modest linkages between them)—as in the teams, departments, and divisions in a company—the adverse consequences of local changes can be restricted to being local. This can allow the system as a whole to evolve more rapidly, because pieces of it that need to adapt can do so without disturbing the entire system.

But that is precisely what most large organizations do *not* do. Even when they do have nested and loosely coupled units in terms of workflow, they typically attempt to impose global uniformity requirements in terms of organization designs on all the sub-units. Many senior managers I have interacted with have no trouble seeing that R&D and sales units will have different organization designs but have a harder time accepting that sales units for two different product lines may also have substantially different designs.

DD strives for an explicit acceptance of 'diversity in designs' within a large organization. This goes beyond the idea that different units doing different kinds of work should have different designs. Rather, I am arguing that even units doing the same kind of work can have different designs, as with the distribution centres in different cities in the FPS example. This is because the people in different units are not identical.

In my People Analytics classes for MBAs, I'm fond of pointing out that people are not randomly assigned into organization designs. Both companies and employees spend enormous efforts in mutual sorting—in finding positions and people that match. In fact, how to improve that match is a major theme of the class! It should therefore surprise no one that a design that works with one set of people may not work with another. The importance of people-contingent design is very well recognized even in the macro-design frameworks such as the Congruence or Star models. I am pushing for taking that recognition seriously, down to the design of the smallest organizational units.

Ensuring Local Participation

Local participation in the formation of local designs (and at least a voice in the process of creating global designs) is the second pillar of the approach I am describing.

The history of top-down attempts at redesigning systems, whether within organizations or at the level of entire countries, is littered with failures arising from ignorance about local conditions.[150] Local participation in decisions is good because relevant knowledge about interdependence, competencies, and constraints is likely to be held locally. Part of that knowledge pertains to how people react to a design. A new organization design creates a new organizational context, and people will react to that in ways that may be difficult for a designer working at arm's length to foresee.[151]

Further, all designs necessarily impose constraints (such as accountability and globally fixed design parameters). But it is one thing to dislike constraints imposed by others versus those voluntarily and collectively accepted based on convincing reasons.

This is why local participation in designing the systems that individuals must eventually live and work in can be so attractive, in addition to the benefits of capturing local knowledge.

The Nobel laureate and economist Elinor Ostrom spent a lifetime studying how rural and agrarian communities governed themselves to use their precious natural resources in a sustainable manner.[152] One of her key findings was the importance of participation in the formulation of governance principles. People are more willing to make a design work when they played a role in formulating it. This idea has made its way quite early into management theory as well. Karl Weick wrote about organizations as self-designing systems, highlighting the power of participation in producing and implementing designs.[153] The socio-technical systems approach to organization design and its variants are popular in the Netherlands as well as the Nordic region,[154] and one of its central pillars again is designing by those who must work within the design. It is the essence of what Paul Adler and Bryan Borys called an 'enabling bureaucracy'.[155]

The two benefits of participative design—of motivation and tapping into local information—also complement each other. An important aspect of local information is knowing how a design will affect human centricity and who better to assess that than the people at the receiving end of the design. A very important advantage, in my view, of participative local designing is that it is unlikely to generate designs that harm human centricity for the group in question.

People can vary enormously in their organizational context preferences (Figure 7). How much autonomy do you need? Sense of connection? Of purpose? Of fairness? With what weights? Rather than trying to measure that heterogeneity and finding a global design that is human-centric for everyone *and* is goal centric, the alternative is to let the micro-organizations that design themselves make their own assessment of what is or is not human-centric, based on the preferences of that group. When the smallest units of design are the micro-organizations (teams and working groups) that design themselves, the appropriate use of data to support this can be best judged by the designers themselves.

For instance, should a team use self-selection for tasks or instead use centralized task allocation via a manager? Should they schedule remote working such that some people show up on the same day or should it be free for all? Does using an LLM improve or worsen the product design work the team does? Should the team use VR technologies for team meetings? These questions can be answered better with data, but what data can be collected and used to answer them should be left as a choice to the team. Decentralized designing allows those who must live in the resulting design to express their preferences about how to use data in a manner they are comfortable with. This is what the team at each distribution centre does in the FPS example.

I do not think I am being naïve in assuming away the possibility of inertia and resistance to data and technology, and there may often have to be some degree of globally imposed data and technology use; rather my point is that a high degree of centralization in such decisions should not be the default. **Decentralized designing is an attempt to 'change the defaults'.** What uses of data would be considered intrusive, and what would be considered useful to improve how a group works—these are decisions that a group's members must have some voice in.

Let me also set a possible concern at rest: the delegation of design to local participants need not mean any loss in accountability. To be clear, in most organizations, and certainly all corporations, legally, the CEO is ultimately accountable and decisions can't really be decentralized the way they can between the centre and states in a federal structure of national government, like in the US or India. Delegation does not mean immunity from accountability. Rather it means that superiors can emphasize holding subordinates accountable for *results*, rather than micro-manage their input actions.

Decentralized designing could operate similarly. While local units are held accountable for results, they have latitude in how to organize to achieve them, subject to a common framework and some global constraints. For instance, each distribution centre in the FPS example still meets KPIs set by the headquarters. One can specify an explicit delegation 'contract' as to which aspects of design are flexible and which ones are not. For instance, the solutions to reward provision and exception handling could be global, but every unit could make its own choices on other dimensions; some tasks such as procurement or hiring could be specified globally, but measuring supplier performance or team building practices could vary significantly.

Let's again contrast the DD approach with the macro-design frameworks. Those were born in a context in which decision rights about how the organization should work were concentrated near the top of the corporate hierarchy, and organization design was seen primarily as a senior management problem. True, they might have delegated operational decisions, but design decisions were not typically delegated and were usually taken at the top. But the enormous variety and complexity of task environments faced by the different parts of an organization today make this approach unviable, and the command-and-control approach to design seems unworkable going forward.[156]

Organization design professionals who used the macro-design frameworks such as the Star and 7S have understood this for a long time, and the sophisticated ones made attempts to incorporate participation and consultative approaches to the formulation of designs. Some go to the extent of using the frameworks symbolically, as totems around which different stakeholders come together to have engaged and serious discussions. This may be pragmatic, but seriously under-utilizes the power of organizational design thinking beyond the capacity to foster legitimacy and engagement.

In contrast, decentralized designing allows for an approach to designing where different parts of an organization might each have different designs (i.e. different solutions to the universal problems), but all operate within a common global framework, such as a set of shared constraints on possible sets of solutions.

Algorithm-Assisted Design

The third pillar of decentralized designing is the use of AI algorithms to support participative design through traditional Big Data, predictive analytics, as well as generative AI.

I believe this is possible because of a powerful implication of the universal problems of organizing (UPO) framework (see Chapter 4): even though the designs can vary widely across units, *all can use the same design tools*. This is because every part of an organization will confront the exact same five UPOs, even though the same solutions will not apply everywhere. For instance, one could imagine every unit within an organization using AI-enabled tools that can help them design themselves. Each unit must solve the universal problems of task division, task allocation, reward distribution, information provision, and exception handling. There may be global, organization-wide constraints on the space from within which solutions can be used, but in DD, there should still be latitude for each unit to participatively decide on locally appropriate solutions from within this defined space.

Two challenges immediately arise. First, will local units have the competence to design themselves? As we have seen (Chapter 4), what makes organization design so challenging is the vast design space of possibilities, and the need to search that space with a combination of theory and evidence to find solutions that are suitable for specific contexts. Second, how can we ensure local designs are consistent with the global design framework? If they are not, we may get a mess of conflicts and inconsistencies.

AI algorithms can help solve both problems. Inspired by AI tools in drug discovery, we can build GenAI tools that can help humans search through the vast space of OD solutions in a theoretically guided manner. My collaborator Nghi Truong and I developed the 'Eunomicon', an application based on large language models to do exactly this. Named after the goddess in the Greek pantheon of good order and governance, the Eunomicon itself is not a piece of software. Rather, it a body of knowledge that we have engineered through careful trials and much thought, that turns theoretical ideas like the universal problems of organizing and organizational context preferences into a framework for action. It can be fine-tuned with organization-specific knowledge, layered onto any Large Language Model and the result is a customized 'Smart-Bot' that acts as a coach and co-pilot for organization design.

Every self-designing team in a large complex organization can use a technology like the Eunomicon to search the space of possible designs that are locally most appropriate to them, subject to constraints created by the global design that can be set into the system. Eunomicon can also advise users on what data to collect, and how to analyse it to make design decisions. When placed on an appropriately powerful LLM, it can also conduct the analysis with that data—regression analysis, A/B testing, natural language processing, etc. We have also built a design evaluation process, where a committee of AI personas, each primed with different criteria, can offer an evaluation of any proposed design. We can even build a committee of LLMs, each equipped with the knowledge layer of Eunomicon, but each producing different perspectives on the same problem.

Algorithmic systems like the Eunomicon solve both challenges associated with decentralizing design—of ensuring local competence as well as global coherence. Such a system could also be designed to enable peer-to-peer learning among units by identifying those that seemed to face similar underlying design challenges even if they are superficially in very different work contexts (a problem similar to recommending books on Amazon or movies on Netflix). The difference is that the data will have been generated with the full cognizance and participation of the units designing themselves.

Conclusion

The three pillars of decentralized designing—differentiated local designs, local participation, and algorithmic assistance—are not only individually useful, but they also reinforce each other (Figure 15). Participation helps ensure that the local designs properly match local conditions. Those who must live in a design ultimately know more about local constraints, as well as about their own attitudes to the design, and to what extent it satisfies their organizational context preferences. Localizing design on the other hand increase the value of participation, for the same reasons. Local designing also increases the benefits of algorithmic support in the design process. Algorithmic assistance for design enables local participation by offering the technical competence necessary for design, while also ensuring coherence between local and global designs.

Both data and AI can of course be used to support centralized, top-down design efforts too. It is all too tempting to aggregate data to one location (usually the CEO's office) and try to make the magic of central planning work, this time with algorithms. A core concern of this book has been about how to protect ourselves from the assaults on human centricity such an approach could produce. I believe with decentralized designing, or something like it, we can flip the problem on its head and turn the potential problems posed by algorithms into a solution.

Ultimately, decentralized designing is a proposal to use digital algorithms to support and stitch together a myriad experiments in how to organize, led by humans but supported by (AI) algorithms.

Let the experiments begin!

Acknowledgements

My thanks go, first, to my research collaborators. Every idea in
this book comes either directly from my research with them or
has been shaped enormously in conversations with them. Our
joint work is cited throughout the book.

A panel of extremely thoughtful and helpful readers looked
over drafts of every chapter and talked through various key ideas
(sometimes both). Their comments and my responses made
writing this book a truly interactive and engaging experience for
me. I felt like I was in constant, stimulating conversation with
them, at least in my mind.

In alphabetical order, these kind souls are Ralf Buechsenschuss,
Julien Clement, Marie Girschewski, Piyush Gulati, Martin
Gonzalez, Vivianna Fang He, Tianyu He, Helge Klapper, Özgecan
Koçak, Sun Young Lee, Arianna Marchetti, Joel Nielsen, Marlo
Raveendran, Markus Reitzig, Yash Raj Shrestha, Bart Vanneste,
and Maciej Workiewicz. Thank you ever so much.

I wrote this book while on sabbatical (the first I ever took
in my career!). My thanks to INSEAD for supporting it. I am
grateful for research funding from the Desmarais Fund and the
chair professorship endowed by Roland Berger at INSEAD.

A special thanks to my sabbatical hosts Glenn Carroll and
Jesper Sørensen at Stanford University, and Paola Criscuolo
and Kevin Corley at Imperial College London. I was also
fortunate to be made welcome by Henrik Jensen and colleagues
at the Complexity & Networks Group at Imperial College. The

intellectual and physical ecologies of Stanford and Imperial are huge sources of inspiration in themselves—one can't but help think on a different scale and scope when immersed in them.

I hope the result is at least a fraction as useful to others as producing it has been enjoyable for me.

Notes

Chapter 1: What This Book Is About

1 Harari, Y. N. (2015). *Sapiens*. Harper.

2 Piketty, T. (2020). *Capital and Ideology*. Harvard University Press.

3 Howard, J. L. (2024). Guaranteed Basic Income from the Perspective of Self-Determination Theory. *Journal of Management Studies*. https://doi.org/10.1111/joms.13075.

    Also see Gilbert, R., Murphy, N. A., Stepka, A., Barrett, M. & Worku, D. (2018). Would a Basic Income Guarantee Reduce the Motivation to Work? An Analysis of Labor Responses in 16 Trial Programs. *Basic Income Studies*, 13(2): 1–12. https://doi.org/10.1515/bis-2018-0011.

4 Richard Bartle created a widely used taxonomy of what motivates video game players; it is analogous to the OCPs I describe in this chapter. See Bartle taxonomy of player types on Wikipedia.

5 Fox, R. (1991). *Encounter with Anthropology*. New York, NY: Harcourt Brace Jovanovich.

6 Galbraith, J. R. (1973). *Designing Complex Organizations*. Reading, MA: Addison-Wesley.

    Peters, T., & Waterman, R. H. (1982). *In search of excellence*. Harper and Row.

    Burton, R. M., DeSanctis, G., & Obel, B. (2006). *Organizational Design: A Step-by-Step Approach*. Cambridge University Press.

Nadler, D., & Tushman, M. A Model for Diagnosing Organizational Behavior. *Organizational Dynamics* 9, no. 2 (autumn 1980): 35–51.

Laloux, F. (2014). *Reinventing Organizations: A Guide to Creating Organizations Inspired by the Next Stage of Human Consciousness.* Brussels: Nelson Parker.

Hamel, G., & Zanini, M. (2020). *Humanocracy: Creating Organizations as Amazing as the People Inside Them.* Harvard Business Review Press.

Foss N. J., & Klein, P. G. (2022). *Why Managers Matter: The Perils of the Bossless Company.* UK: Hachette.

Reitzig, M. (2022). *Get Better at Flatter: A Guide to Shaping and Leading Organizations with Less Hierarchy.* Switzerland AG: Springer Nature.

Chapter 2: What Is Changing

7   For latest figures, see Our World in Data: Artificial intelligence. https://ourworldindata.org/artificial-intelligence.

8   I have described these trends in more detail in two papers: What has changed? The Impact of Covid Pandemic on the Technology and Innovation Management Research Agenda (G. George, K. Lakhani, and P. Puranam, *Journal of Management Studies*, 2020). https://doi.org/10.1111/joms.12634.

Adner, Ron, Phanish Puranam, & Feng Zhu. What Is Different About Digital Strategy? From Quantitative to Qualitative Change. *Strategy Science* 4, no. 4 (December 2019): 253–261.

9   This section draws on my paper What Is Different About Digital Strategy? From Quantitative to Qualitative Change (with Adner, R., & Zhu, F. *Strategy Science*, 2019).

10 For instance, see: Barrero, J. M., Bloom, N., & Davis, S. J. (2021). Why Working from Home Will Stick. *National Bureau of Economic Research.* https://doi.org/10.3386/w28731.

11 Katie Collins (8 March 2022). Twitter Bot Exposes Gender Pay Gap of Companies Tweeting About International Women's Day. *CNET*. https://www.cnet.com/culture/internet/twitter-bot-exposes-gender-pay-gap-of-companies-tweeting-about-international-womens-day/.

12 The difference often persists even after accounting for the smaller number of women in the organization than men. This is useful to adjust for if there is a tendency for ties to be of the same sex.

13 Herbert A. Simon has been a hero of mine since I was as an engineering sophomore when I first encountered his work, and one of the major regrets of my professional life is that I missed the opportunity (by just a few weeks) of meeting him before he died. This may help the reader understand, if not forgive, my frequent groupie-like references to him and his work.

14 Intelligence is 'an agent's ability to achieve goals in a wide range of environments'. It is associated more generally with reasoning, learning, decision-making, problem-solving, and other higher-order thinking skills. See for instance Legg, S., & Hutter, M. (2007). Universal Intelligence: A Definition of Machine Intelligence. *Minds and Machines*, 17: 391–444.

15 This is a highly simplified account of how supervised machine learning works. For a more detailed but still accessible discussion and comparison with other kinds of machine learning such as unsupervised learning and reinforcement learning, see my paper Algorithm Supported Induction for Building Theory: How Can We Use Prediction Models to Theorize? (with Sreshtha, Y. R., He, V. F., & von Krogh, G. *Organization Science*, 2020)

16 Agrawal, A., Gans, J., & Goldfarb, A. (2018). *Prediction Machines: The Simple Economics of artificial intelligence*. Harvard Business Press.

17 Bender, E. M., Gebru, T., McMillan-Major, A., & Shmitchell, S. (2021). On the Dangers of Stochastic Parrots: Can Language Models Be Too Big? In Proceedings of the 2021 ACM Conference on Fairness, Accountability, and Transparency.

18 If the reference to 'Babel fish' puzzles you, you really must read the *Hitchhiker's Guide to the Galaxy* by Douglas Adams.

19 I use the acronym SPICE to help my students remember the possible applications of ChatGPT: Summarize, build Pseudo-personalities, Ideate, Conversational coding, Evaluate.

20 Kurzweil, R. (2005). *The Singularity Is Near: When Humans Transcend Biology*. Viking.

21 Puranam, P. (2024). Designing Artificial Organizations. *Medium*. https://phanishpuranam.medium.com/designing-artificial-organizations-7a165f270b4c.

22 Relatively recent papers by leading scholars that offered this view include:

   Acemoglu, K. D., & Restrepo, P. (2019). Automation and New Tasks: How technology displaces and reinstates labor. *Journal of Economic Perspectives*, 33(2): 3–30.

   Argote, L., Lee, S., & Park, J. (2020). Organizational Learning Processes and Outcomes: Major Findings and Future Research Directions. *Management Science*, 67(9): 5399–5429. https://doi.org/10.1287/mnsc.2020.3693.

23 Autor, D. (2022). The labour market impacts of technological change : from unbridled enthusiasm to qualified optimism to vast uncertainty. *National Bureau of Economic Research*. https://nber.org.

   Acemoglu, D., & Johnson, S. (2023). *Power and Progress: Our Thousand-Year Struggle Over Technology and Prosperity*. Basic Books.

24 Susskind, D. (2020). *A World Without Work: Technology, Automation, and How We Should Respond*. Penguin Books.

25 Labour market conditions and employee's working conditions inside organizations are of course correlated, and I do discuss this linkage (which can take surprising forms) in the next chapter.

26 Jack E. Steele on Wikipedia. I did consider 'cyborg' but discarded it because of its negative connotations (think Darth Vader in *Star Wars* or the Borg in *Star Trek*); and 'orgarithm' was of surpassing ugliness.

27 Vanneste, B.S., & Puranam, P. (2024). Artificial intelligence, Trust and Perceptions of Agency. *Academy of Management Review*, Forthcoming.

28 A number of examples can be found here:
    https://cvviz.com/product/resume-screening/ (Accessed 7 March 2023).
    https://www.nellyssecurity.com/blog/articles/video-surveillance/what-is-deep-learning-ai-and-why-is-it-important-for-video-surveillance (Accessed 11 February 2023).
    https://openai.com/blog/chatgpt (Accessed 23 January 2023).
    https://techhq.com/2019/04/ibm-could-be-a-model-for-hr-in-the-ai-age/ (Accessed 27 January 2023).
    https://www.cnbc.com/2019/04/03/ibm-ai-can-predict-with-95-percent-accuracy-which-employees-will-quit.html (Accessed 10 March 2023).

29 Yann LeCun on LinkedIn: I've made that point before. https://www.linkedin.com/posts/yann-lecun_ive-made-that-point-before-llm-1e13-activity-7156484065603280896-QH63.

30 McKinsey Global Institute. (2024). A new future of work: The race to deploy AI and raise skills in Europe and beyond. https://www.mckinsey.com/mgi/our-research/a-new-future-of-work-the-race-to-deploy-ai-and-raise-skills-in-europe-and-beyond.

31 Howard, J. L. (2024). Guaranteed Basic Income from the Perspective of Self-Determination Theory. *Journal of Management Studies*. https://doi.org/10.1111/joms.13075.

Chapter 3: What Remains Constant

32 Any assumptions about OCPs I make for my arguments here, such as completeness, transitivity, non-satiation, convexity, and stability should be treated as conjectures subject to empirical verification rather than axiomatic.

33 Economists use 'meaning' as an umbrella term to capture non-monetary incentives and non-pecuniary benefits—all the positive 'workplace attributes beyond income'. In a recent and influential review, Casser and Meier (2018) summarize the empirical findings as follows: 'Work represents much more than simply earning an income: for many people, work is a source of meaning.' The authors review a large number of studies, both correlational as well as field experimental that together paint a compelling case for the two propositions I outlined—people care about 'workplace attributes other than income' and will give up salary for them. See:

Cassar, L., & Meier, S. (2018). Nonmonetary Incentives and the Implications of Work as a Source of Meaning. *Journal of Economic Perspectives*, 32(3).

34 See the overview of Firm Specific Incentives in Kryscynski, D., Coff, R., & Campbell, B. (2021). Charting a path between firm-specific incentives and human capital-based competitive advantage. *Strategic Management Journal*, 42(2): 386–412.

35 The technical terms for this and closely related problems include 'contractual incompleteness', 'unobservability of effort', and, in the world of AI, 'the alignment problem'. In each case the challenge is that the principal cannot hope to specify exactly and in advance what they want the agent to do. This is the reason that 'working to rule' (aka a 'slowdown') is an effective form of industrial action.

36 See Edmans, A. (2016). 28 Years of Stock Market Data Shows a Link Between Employee Satisfaction and Long-Term

Value. *Harvard Business Review*. https://hbr.org/2016/03/28-years-of-stock-market-data-shows-a-link-between-employee-satisfaction-and-long-term-value.

37 See, for instance, Gartenberg, C. (2023). The Contingent Relationship Between Purpose and Profits. *Strategy Science*, 8(2), 256–269.

38 In their extensive review, Casser and Meier (2018) also found that there appears to be a non-trivial minority of people who seem not to care for anything except money from their organizational contexts. It is not clear if this represents poor measurement of their OCPs or if perhaps they satisfy their OCPs in non-work-related organizations.

39 Universal Declaration of Human Rights. United Nations. https://www.un.org/en/about-us/universal-declaration-of-human-rights.

40 I borrowed this brilliant analogy from Jonathan Haidt, who used it to explain his Moral Foundations theory. Haidt, J. (2012). *The Righteous Mind: Why Good People are Divided by Politics and Religion*. London: Penguin.

41 For a concise overview of 'multi-level selection theory', which is the relevant set of ideas that explain the universal structure of our preferences for organizational contexts, please see Chapter 1 of Atkins, P. W. B., Wilson, D. S., & Hayes, S. C. (2019). *Prosocial: Using evolutionary science to build productive, equitable, and collaborative groups*. Context Press/New Harbinger Publications.

The architect of modern muti-level selection theory, David S. Wilson, wrote a landmark paper in 2007 with E. O. Wilson—a prominent biologist who was formerly a critic of the theory. This paper converged their thinking to the point where it is now mainstream in evolutionary biology and is our current best explanation for the evolutionary roots of human behaviour in groups. The quote from Wilson and

Wilson that summarizes this synthesis elegantly is from their paper: Wilson, D. S., & Wilson, E. O. (2007). Rethinking the Theoretical Foundation of Sociobiology. *The Quarterly Review of Biology*, 82(4): 327–348.

42   Most readers are probably aware of Maslow's hierarchy of needs. However, once we move past basic physiological needs, our understanding of the higher-level needs has advanced considerably through research. My review led me to adopt Self-determination Theory (SDT) by Richard Ryan and Edward Deci (2017, 2020) as an overarching framework to understand universal human motivators in group contexts. In my view, SDT is the best theoretical synthesis we have today about a universal theory of human motivation in organizations. The motivators it identifies are likely to be functional universals in the terminology of Norenzayan and Heine 2005. These motivators exist across cultures, but are not equally accessible, even though all perform the same function (increase intrinsic motivation).

The empirical support for SDT's predictions is strong. Meta-analytic (i.e., 'studies of studies') reviews strongly support the importance of the intrinsic motivators identified by SDT for human well-being (Bradshaw et al, 2023; Van den Broeck et al, 2021). Casser and Meier's review of evidence (2018) on the drivers of non-financial, non-pecuniary sources of motivation decomposed them into four components. Three of those are based directly on Deci and Ryan (2020)—namely autonomy, competence, and relatedness. The fourth is 'mission' or collective purpose which is the fifth dimension on my list. Nikolova and Cnossen (2020) use data from across three waves of the European Working Condition Survey and document that 'autonomy, competence, and relatedness are about 4.6 times more important for meaningfulness at work than compensation, benefits, career advancement, job insecurity, and working hours. Relatedness, which reflects supportive relationships with colleagues and superiors, emerges as the most important factor for work meaningfulness.' The triad of autonomy, competence, and relatedness together explain about 60 per cent of the variation in perceptions of work meaningfulness, which in turn is strongly predictive of absenteeism, skills training, and retirement plans.

Bradshaw, E. L., Conigrave, J. H., Steward, B. A., Ferber, K. A., Parker, P. D., & Ryan, R. M. (2023). A meta-analysis of the dark side of the American dream: Evidence for the universal wellness costs of prioritizing extrinsic over intrinsic goals. *Journal of Personality and Social Psychology*, 124(4): 873–899. https://doi.org/10.1037/pspp0000431.

Van den Broeck, A., Howard, J. L., Van Vaerenbergh, Y., Leroy, H., & Gagné, M. (2021). Beyond intrinsic and extrinsic motivation: A meta-analysis on self-determination theory's multidimensional conceptualization of work motivation. *Organizational Psychology Review*, 11(3): 240–273. https://doi.org/10.1177/20413866211006173

Nikolova, M., & Cnossen, F. (2020). What Makes Work Meaningful and Why Economists Should Care About it. IZA Discussion Paper No. 13112. http://dx.doi.org/10.2139/ssrn.3568317.

Norenzayan, A., & Heine, S. J. (2005). Psychological Universals: What Are They and How Can We Know? *Psychological Bulletin*, 131(5): 763.

Ryan, R. M., & Deci, E. L. (2017). Self-determination theory: Basic psychological needs in motivation, development, and wellness. *The Guilford Press*. https://doi.org/10.1521/978.14625/28806.

Ryan, R. M., & Deci, E. L. (2020). Intrinsic and extrinsic motivation from a self-determination theory perspective: Definitions, theory, practices, and future directions. *Contemporary Educational Psychology*, 61, Article 101860. https://doi.org/10.1016/j.cedpsych.2020.101860.

43 Here is a summary of the broader literatures (as well as SDT) from which I have drawn the six fundamental dimensions along which to measure OCPs.

Autonomy occurs as a fundamental motivator in multiple research traditions: in Self-determination Theory (SDT) (Deci and Ryan, 2002; Ryan and Deci, 2017), in the literatures on decision rights (Bartling, Fehr and Herz, 2014), task design (Hackman and Oldham, 1976), in the literature on control aversion, in Schwartz's Universal Values Framework as self-direction (2007), and as the hierarchy-subversion dimension in Haidt's moral foundations framework (2012).

Competence is the need to feel capable and effective at actions in SDT (Ryan and Deci, 2017), and is closely related if not identical to the 'need for achievement' in McClelland (1961) and 'achievement values' in the Universal Values Framework (Schwartz, 2007). Both McClelland and Schwartz in their respective frameworks explicitly include both the sense of satisfaction with being capable and effective as well as the resulting acclaim and appreciation from others as part of the intrinsic motivation one derives from competence.

Relatedness as feeling connected to others and forming meaningful relationships with them is central not only to SDT (Deci and Ryan, 2000) but also occurs as the 'need for affiliation' in McClelland (1961) and Schwartz's Universal Values framework (2007). It is also argued to provide a source of intrinsic motivation.

Fairness as a contextual attribute that promotes intrinsic motivation appears in the literature on inequity aversion (Fehr and Schmidt, 1999), fairness preference (Larkin, Pierce and Gino 2012), and as a basic element of moral foundations theory Haidt (2012).

Collective purpose refers to the perception that an individual's efforts contribute to the goals of the immediate group (e.g., the firm). An interesting case is when those goals contribute to the welfare of broader groups (e.g., segments of society). There is some evidence that employees will accept lower wages, display greater engagement and lower attrition if their employers invest in Corporate Social Responsibility activities (Cassar and Meier, 2018). Social identity theory argues that experiencing a sense of collective purpose is intrinsically motivating, and also increases in-group loyalty and altruism even when the group level goal is competition with other groups rather than their welfare (Tajfel and Turner, 1979; 1986).

Novelty (also referred to as curiosity in some sources) is the individual's perception of experiencing or doing something new, including switching things up in different combination (Loewenstein, 1994; Bagheri and Milyavskaya, 2020). Providing opportunities for fulfilling curiosity is argued to be a source of intrinsic motivation, though different scholars treat it somewhat differently (e.g., it is considered a subset of self-direction for Schwartz, 2007, who distinguishes it from stimulation.)

The first three (autonomy, competence, and relatedness) are the primary dimensions of OCPs and are drawn directly from decades long research in social and evolutionary psychology, summarized SDT (Deci and Ryan, 2020). The next three dimensions (fairness, collective purpose, and curiosity) have also been found to be important but appear to contribute to or be built upon the primary dimensions.

Bagheri, L., & Milyavskaya, M. (2020). Novelty–variety as a candidate basic psychological need: New evidence across three studies. *Motivation and Emotion*, 44(1): 32–53. https://doi.org/10.1007/s11031-019-09807-4

Bartling, B., Fehr, E., & Herz, H. (2014). The Intrinsic Value of Decision Rights. *Econometrica*, 82(6): 2005–2039. http://www.jstor.org/stable/43616906.

Cassar, L., & Meier, S. (2018). Nonmonetary Incentives and the Implications of Work as a Source of Meaning. *Journal of Economic Perspectives*, 32(3): 215–38. https://doi.org/10.1257/jep.32.3.215

Deci, E. L., & Ryan, R. M. (2000). The 'What' and 'Why' of Goal Pursuits: Human Needs and the Self-Determination of Behavior. *Psychological Inquiry*, 11(4): 227–68. https://doi.org/10.1207/S15327965PLI1104_01.

Fehr, E., & Schmidt, K. M. (1999). A Theory of Fairness, Competition, and Cooperation. *The Quarterly Journal of Economics*, 114(3): 817–868. https://doi.org/10.1162/003355399556151

Hackman, J. R., & Oldham, G. R. (1976). Motivation through the design of work: test of a theory. *Organizational Behavior and Human Performance*, 16(2): 250–279. https://doi.org/10.1016/0030-5073(76)90016-7.

Haidt, J. (2012). *The Righteous Mind: Why Good People are Divided by Politics and Religion.* London: Penguin.

Larkin, I., Pierce, L., & Gino, F. (2012). The Psychological Costs of Pay-for-Performance: Implications for the Strategic Compensation of Employees. *Strategic Management Journal*, 33(10): 1194–1214. https://doi.org/10.1002/smj.1974

Loewenstein, G. (1994). The psychology of curiosity: A review and reinterpretation. *Psychological Bulletin*, 116(1): 75–98. https://doi.org/10.1037/0033-2909.116.1.75

McClelland, D.C. (1961). *The Achieving Society.* Van Nostrand.

Ryan, R. M., & Deci, E. L. (2017). Self-determination theory: Basic psychological needs in motivation, development, and wellness. *The Guilford Press.* https://doi.org/10.1521/978.14625/28806.

Schwartz, S. H. (2007). Basic human values: Theory, measurement, and applications. *Revue Française de Sociologie*, 47(4): 929.

Tajfel, H. & Turner, J. C. (1986). The Social Identity Theory of Intergroup Behavior. In: Worchel, S. & Austin, W. G. (Eds.) *Psychology of Intergroup Relations*. Chicago, IL: Nelson-Hall.

Tajfel, H. (1974). Social identity and intergroup behaviour. *Social Science Information*, 13(2): 65–93. https://doi.org/10.1177/053901847401300204.

Zuckerman, M. (1979). *Sensation Seeking: Beyond the Optimal Level of Arousal*. Hillsdale, NJ: Lawrence Erlbaum Associates.

44 See for instance the literature on control aversion, e.g., Rudorf, S., Schmelz, K., Baumgartner, T., Wiest, R., Fischbacher, U., & Knoch, D. (2018). Neural Mechanisms Underlying Individual Differences in Control-Averse Behavior. *The Journal of Neuroscience*, 38(22): 5196–5208. https://doi.org/10.1523/JNEUROSCI.0047-18.2018

45 Marchetti, A., & Puranam, P. (2022). Organizational cultural strength as the negative cross-entropy of mindshare: a measure based on descriptive text. *Humanities and Social Sciences Communications*, 9(135). https://doi.org/10.1057/s41599-022-01152-1.

46 See: https://www.mckinsey.com/featured-insights/sustainable-inclusive-growth/chart-of-the-day/what-generational-divide.

As well as: Twenge, J. (2023). *Generations: The Real Differences Between Gen Z, Millennials, Gen X, Boomers, and Silents—and What They Mean for America's Future*. New York: Atria Books.

47 World Values Survey: Round Seven (2017–2020): Haerpfer, C., Inglehart, R., Moreno, A., Welzel, C., Kizilova, K., Diez-Medrano, J., Lagos, M., Norris, P., Ponarin, E., & Puranen, B. (Eds.). (2022). World Values Survey: Round Seven – Country-Pooled Datafile Version 6.0. Madrid, Spain &

Vienna, Austria: JD Systems Institute & WVSA Secretariat. https://doi.org/10.14281/18241.1

48 Anonymous. (2015). Digital Taylorism. *The Economist*, 416(8955), 63.

49 For instance, see the case of Patagonia in Chapter 6, *Get Better at Flatter* by Markus Reitzig.

50 Akerlof, G. A. (1984). Gift Exchange and Efficiency-Wage Theory: Four Views. *The American Economic Review*, 74(2): 79–83. https://www.jstor.org/stable/1816334.

51 Henaway, M. (2023). Amazon's distribution space: constructing a 'labour fix' through digital Taylorism and corporate Keynesianism. *ZFW – Advances in Economic Geography*, 67(4): 202–216. https://doi.org/10.1515/zfw-2022-0017.

52 Ferreras, I., Battilana, J., & Méda, D. (2022). *Democratize Work: The Case for Reorganizing the Economy*. University of Chicago Press.
   Also see: Young-Hyman, T., Magne, N., & Kruse, D. L. (2022). A Real Utopia Under What Conditions? The Economic and Social Benefits of Workplace Democracy in Knowledge-Intensive Industries. *Organization Science*, 34(4): 1353–1382.

53 Cameron, L. D. (2024). The Making of the "Good Bad" Job: How Algorithmic Management Manufactures Consent Through Constant and Confined Choices. *Administrative Science Quarterly*, 69(2): 458–514. https://doi.org/10.1177/00018392241236163.

54 Vanneste, B., & Puranam, P. Artificial intelligence, Trust, and Perceptions of Agency. Academy of Management Review (In press).

55 McKinsey Global Institute. (2024). Help wanted: Charting the challenge of tight labor markets in advanced economies. https://www.mckinsey.com/mgi/our-research/help-wanted-charting-the-challenge-of-tight-labor-markets-in-advanced-economies.

56 Adler, P. S., & Borys, B. (1996). Two types of bureaucracy: Enabling and Coercive. *Administrative Science Quarterly*, 41(1): 61–89.

Chapter 4: Algorithms and Organizing

57 Brynjolfsson, E., & McAfee, A. (2014). *The Second Machine Age: Work, Progress, and Prosperity in a Time of Brilliant Technologies.* New York: W.W. Norton & Company.

    Hernandez, K., Faith, B., Prieto Martín, P., & Ramalingam, B. (2016). The Impact of Digital Technology on Economic Growth and Productivity, and its Implications for Employment and Equality: An Evidence Review. *IDS Evidence Report 207*.

58 Bloom, N., Sadun, R., & Reenen, J. V. (2012). Americans Do IT Better: US Multinationals and the Productivity Miracle. *American Economic Review*, 102(1): 167–201. https:doi.org/10.1257/aer.102.1.167.

    Brynjolfsson, E., Jin, W., & McElheran, K. (2021). The Power of Prediction: Predictive Analytics, Workplace Complements, and Business Performance. *Business Economics*, 56(4): 217–239.

59 Gartner Research. (2021). Understanding Gartner's Hype Cycles. https://www.gartner.com/en/documents/4003232.

60 Organizational Design Community. What is Organization Design? (orgdesigncomm.com)

61 Puranam, P., Alexy, O., & Reitzig, M. (2014). What's 'New' About New Forms of Organizing? *Academy of Management Review*, 39 (2): 162–180. http://www.jstor.org/stable/43699235.

62 Puranam, P. (2018). *The Microstructure of Organizations.* Oxford University Press. https://doi.org/10.1093/oso/9780199672363.001.0001.

63 Puranam, P., & Clement, J. (2023). The Organizational Analytics E-book Ver 2.0. (orgdesigncomm.com)

64 Puranam, P. (2018). *The Microstructure of Organizations*. Oxford University Press.

65 Henderson, R. M., & Clark, K. B. (1990). Architectural Innovation: The Reconfiguration of Existing Product Technologies and the Failure of Established Firms. *Administrative Science Quarterly*, 35(1): 9–30. These authors argued that organizational practices mediate and not only moderate the effect of technology on productivity.

66 Puranam, P. (2024). Designing Artificial Organizations. *Medium.* https://phanishpuranam.medium.com/designing-artificial-organizations-7a165f270b4c.

67 To illustrate how large design spaces can be, let's consider just two of the UPOs—reward provision and task allocation—in some detail. For simplicity, we will consider only one dimension, financial incentives, under reward provision (i.e., we are ignoring the OCPs for now—these are important but ignoring them does not detract from the point being made here). Researchers have documented that financial incentives vary in their depth and breadth. The extent to which the rewards to a person depend on how they perform captures the depth of incentives. The extent to which the rewards to a person depend on the performance of others (such as their team or the company) captures the breadth of incentives. Increasing depth of incentives (e.g., low base salary and high fraction of pay for performance schemes) can increase motivation but imposes more risk, because the person's performance may not be completely under their control. Increasing breadth of incentives (e.g., using group level incentives) can promote cooperation to capture synergies but can also increase the risk of free riding.

We can thus see that there are at least four mutually exclusive points on the financial incentive dimension—high-

high, high-low, low-high, and low-low in terms of breadth and depth.

Now, let's consider task allocation, again focusing on a single dimension—the basis for matching individuals to tasks. We know that there are three types of matching criteria: skill match, preference-match, and random. Under skill match, task allocation is based on matching individuals with the required skills to the required tasks. This is the most common approach and enhances efficiency. Under preference-match, individuals are assigned tasks they would enjoy doing. This method assumes that when members are assigned tasks they are interested in, they are more likely to be motivated and perform well. Under random allocation, task allocation is based on random assignment, without considering factors such as skills or preferences. This method can promote fairness and prevent favouritism but may not result in the most efficient or motivating task allocation.

Just considering one dimension each of these two fundamental problems (reward distribution and task allocation), we can see there are already at least 12 possible combinations of solutions (4*3): 12 designs that vary on just these two dimensions. Not all combinations will perform equally well.

We can guess that some combinations look promising, such as preference-matched task allocation with low depth and low breadth incentives (e.g., fixed salary). The intrinsic motivation generated by doing what is liked can compensate for the absence of other strong forms of incentives. With other combinations we will not know till we have tried them because performance consequences will be context specific. For instance, neither of the high depth incentive types will probably work with random allocation if the context is one where people vary in what they are skilled at. This is because individuals highly skilled at one task assigned at random to another at which they are not highly skilled will suffer the full consequences of underperformance under deep incentives. But in a context where skill differences are modest, this may not be true.

68 Leonardi, P. M., & Leavell, V. (2024). How the map becomes the territory: prediction, performativity and the process of taking digital twins for granted. *Journal of Organization Design*, 14(1): 1–16;.

Bail, C. (2023). Out of One, Many: Using Language Models to Simulate Human Samples. *Political Analysis*, 31(3): 337–351.

69 Puranam, P., & Clement, J. (2023). *The Organizational Analytics E-book* Ver 2.0. (orgdesigncomm.com).

70 A widely used thumb rule is to have at least thirty units each in treatment and control groups, but this number can vary (upwards or downwards) based on how weak or strong the effect of the treatment is likely to be on the performance measures.

71 This is called the Stable Unit Treatment Value Assumption (SUTVA).

72 Lee, E., & Puranam, P. (2016). The implementation imperative: Why one should implement even imperfect strategies perfectly. *Strategic Management Journal*, 37(8). Wiley Online Library. https://doi.org/10.1002/smj.2414.

73 Park, S., & Puranam, P. (2021). Self-Confirming Biased Beliefs in Organizational "Learning by Doing". https://doi.org/10.1155/2021/8865872.

74 Puranam, P., & Park, S. (2023). Vicarious Learning Without Knowledge Differentials. *Management Science*, 70(5). https://doi.org/10.1287/mnsc.2023.4842.

75 Puranam, P., & Clement, J. (2017). Searching for Structure: Formal Organization Design as a Guide to Network Evolution. *Management Science*, 64(8). https://doi.org/10.1287/mnsc.2017.2807.

Puranam, P. & Swamy, M. (2016). How Initial Representations Shape Coupled Learning Processes. *Organization Science*, 27(2). https://doi.org/10.1287/orsc.2015.1033.

76 Koçak, Ö., Levinthal, D. A., & Puranam, P. (2022). The Dual Challenge of Search and Coordination for Organizational Adaptation: How Structures of Influence Matter. *Organization Science*, 34(2). https://doi.org/10.1287/orsc.2022.1601.

77 Puranam, P., & Clement, J. (2023). *The Organizational Analytics E-book* Ver 2.0. (orgdesigncomm.com).

78 O'Neil, C. (2017). *Weapons of Math Destruction: How Big Data Increases Inequality and Threatens Democracy*. Penguin Books.

79 Take for instance Shoshana Zuboff's devastating takedown of what she calls 'surveillance capitalism', the use of data by tech companies like Google and Microsoft to predict and shape customer behaviour for profit.

Zuboff, S. (2019). *The Age of Surveillance Capitalism: The Fight for a Human Future at the New Frontier of Power*. Profile Books.

80 EU artificial intelligence Act: Up-to-date developments and analyses of the EU AI Act. https://artificialintelligenceact.eu

Chapter 5: Digital Division of Labour

81 Puranam, P. (2018). *The Microstructure of Organizations*, Chapter 3. Oxford University Press.

82 Smith, A. (1776). *The Wealth of Nations*. W. Strahan and T. Cadell.

83 Mintzberg, H. (1979). *The Structuring of Organizations*. Prentice-Hall, Englewood Cliffs.

84 Rubin, P (2000) Hierarchy. *Human Nature*, 11(3): 259–279. https://doi.org/10.1007/s12110-000-1013-3

85 Yuval Noah Harari argued that it makes sense to see agriculture as the domestication of humans by wheat. Lured by the

convenience of a reliable and scalable food source, humans changed their lifestyles and began to organize themselves in ways that involved centralization, hierarchy, inequality, and a significant loss of autonomy (not to mention adverse effects on our health). Wheat, in the meantime, has flourished as a species, in large numbers and across all locations.

Harari, Y. N. (2015). *Sapiens*. Harper.

86 Raveendran, M., Puranam, P., & Warglien, M. (2015). Object Salience in the Division of Labor: Experimental Evidence. *Management Science*, 62(7). https://doi.org/10.1287/mnsc.2015.2216.

87 Cameron, L. D. (2024). The Making of the "Good Bad" Job: How Algorithmic Management Manufactures Consent Through Constant and Confined Choices. *Administrative Science Quarterly*, 69(2): 458–514. https://doi.org/10.1177/00018392241236163.

88 For a thoughtful critique, see Anthony, C., Bechky, B. A., & Fayard, A. L. (2023). "Collaborating" with AI: Taking a System View to Explore the Future of Work. *Organization Science*, 34(5): 1672–1694. https://doi.org/10.1287/orsc.2022.1651.

89 These are known as Universal Approximation Theorems.

90 Puranam, P., & Vanneste, B. (2016). *Corporate Strategy: Tools for Analysis and Decision-Making*. Cambridge University Press.

91 Puranam, P., Gulati, R., & Bhattacharya, S. (2013). How much to make and how much to buy? An analysis of optimal plural sourcing strategies. *Strategic Management Journal*, 34(10): 1145–1161. https://doi.org/10.1002/smj.2063.

92 Ethiraj, S., & Puranam, P. (2004). The Distribution of R&D Effort in Systemic Industries: Implications for Competitive Advantage. Emerald Insight.

93 Kumar, N., & Puranam, P. (2011). *India Inside: The Emerging Innovation Challenge to the West*. Harvard Business Review Press.

94 Raveendran, M., Puranam, P., & Warglien, M. (2021). Division of Labor Through Self-Selection. *Organization Science*, 33(2). https://doi.org/10.1287/orsc.2021.1449.

95 Consider open-source software development communities, which are the epitome of non-hierarchical self-selection into tasks. Researchers studying open-source communities have speculated that self-selection is aided by high levels of specialization in skills among workers. Specialization may enable entry into the community by letting individuals make specific focused contributions. This assumes that workers are specialized before self-selecting into tasks.

96 Anthony, C., Bechky, B. A., & Fayard, A. (2023). "Collaborating" with AI: Taking a System View to Explore the Future of Work. *Organization Science*, 34(5), 1672–1694. https://doi.org/10.1287/orsc.2022.1651.

97 Choudhary, V., Marchetti, A., Shrestha, Y. R., & Puranam, P. (2023). Human-AI Ensembles: When Can They Work? *Journal of Management*. https://doi.org/10.1177/01492063231194968.

98 This latter result was popularized by James Surowiecki as the 'Wisdom of the Crowd', and Scott Page has given elegant mathematical formulations to explain why it arises. See:

      Surowiecki, J. (2004). *The Wisdom of Crowds: Why the Many Are Smarter Than the Few and How Collective Wisdom Shapes Business, Economies, Societies and Nations.* Doubleday.

      Page, S. E. (2007). *The Difference: How the Power of Diversity Creates Better Groups, Firms, Schools, and Societies.* Princeton University Press.

      Page, S. (2019). Appendix. The Diversity Prediction Theorem. In E. Lewis & N. Cantor (Ed.), *The Diversity Bonus: How Great Teams Pay Off in the Knowledge Economy* (pp. 247–250). Princeton: Princeton University Press.

Chapter 6: Digital Integration of Effort

99 Gintis, H., van Schaik, C. P., & Boehm, C. (2015). Zoon Politikon: The Evolutionary Origins of Human Political Systems. *Current Anthropology*, 56(3): 327–353.

Kelly, R. L. (2013). *The Lifeways of Hunter-Gatherers: The Foraging Spectrum.* Cambridge University Press.

Buss, D. M. (2015). *Evolutionary Psychology: The New Science of the Mind.* New York: Psychology Press.

Smith, J. E., Lacey, E. A., & Hayes, L. D. (2017). Sociality in non-primate mammals. In *Comparative Social Evolution.* Rubenstein, D. R., & Abbot, P. (Eds.) Cambridge University Press. Pp. 284–319.

Van Vugt, M. (2017). Evolutionary psychology: theoretical foundations for the study of organizations. *Journal of Organization Design,* 6(1): 9.

100   A detailed statement can be found in Chapter 6 of my book *The Microstructures of Organizations* (2018), Oxford University Press.

A mathematical treatment can be found in Lee, E., Ilseven, E., & Puranam, P. (2023). Scaling nonhierarchically: A theory of conflict-free organizational growth with limited hierarchical growth. *Strategic Management Journal,* 44(12): 3042–3064. https://doi.org/10.1002/smj.3541.

101   Yuval Noah Harari, the author of *Sapiens* (Harper, 2015), makes a strong case that certain kinds of cultural beliefs that he calls 'shared fictions' or 'collectively imagined realities' act as particularly powerful forces for smoothing. This class of cultural beliefs are inherently scalable because their effectiveness increases with the number of people who hold them. He cites examples like nations, money, human rights, and corporations—once people collectively imagined and behaved as if these abstract fictions were real, they became immensely powerful cultural constructs for aligning perspectives and enabling mass cooperation.

102   This idea comes from Lawrence and Lorsch (1967). A formal analysis of the implications for smoothing can be found in Kretchmer and Puranam (2008).

Lawrence, P. R., & Lorsch, J. W. (1967). *Organization and Environment.* Boston, MA: Harvard Business School, Division of Research.

Kretschmer, T., & Puranam, P. (2008). Integration Through Incentives Within Differentiated Organizations. *Organization Science,* 19(6): 860–875.

103 One might think of voting as a procedure through which large groups of people can reach agreement. But to agree on voting as a procedure and to abide by its outcomes is itself not straightforward.

104 Antonopoulos, A. M. (2017). *Mastering Bitcoin: Programming the Open Blockchain.* USA: O'Reilly Media, Inc.

105 He, V. F., & Puranam, P. (2023). Some Challenges for the "New Daoism": A Comment on Klima Dao. *Journal of Organization Design,* 12(4): 293–295.

106 Shaikh, M., & Vaast, E. (2023). Algorithmic Interactions in Open Source Work. *Information Systems Research,* 34(2): 744–765.

Srikanth, K., & Puranam, P. (2014). The Firm as a Coordination System: Evidence from Software Services Offshoring. *Organization Science,* 25(4): 1253–1271.

107 Patton, S. (2023). New ways Microsoft Copilot and Viva are transforming the employee experience. *Microsoft Community Hub.* https://techcommunity.microsoft.com/t5/microsoft-viva-blog/new-ways-microsoft-copilot-and-viva-are-transforming-the/ba-p/3982293.

108 Ketkar, H. (2019). Automation and its Discontents: The Impact of Cognitive Task Automation on Organizational Innovation. (Working paper.)

109 Lambert, B., Caza, B. B., Reid, E., & Ashford, S. (2023). Working in isolation can pose mental health challenges – here's what anyone can learn from how gig workers have adapted. *The Conversation.* https://

theconversation.com/working-in-isolation-can-pose-mental-health-challenges-heres-what-anyone-can-learn-from-how-gig-workers-have-adapted-194712.

110 Minervini, M., Murph, D., & Puranam, P. (2020). Remote Work Doesn't Have to Mean All-Day Video Calls. *Harvard Business Review*.

111 Even when two people are interactively working on the same program, it is much more useful for them to have a view of each other's screen to see what they are manipulating than it is to see each other's faces. Making real-time work visible across locations is another powerful means of smoothing interactions.

112 Kumar, N., & Puranam, P. (2011). *India Inside: The Emerging Innovation Challenge to the West*. Boston, MA: Harvard Business Review Press.

113 These are classified as "Collaborative Work Management" tools by Gartner (*Market Guide for Collaborative Work Management*, 4 January 2023, ID G00761298, www.gartner.com/en/documents/4022601). They include tools like Atlassian Jira, Smartsheet, Clarizen, Asana, and Monday.com.

114 He, V. F., & Puranam, P. (2022). Organising in the Metaverse: Five FAQs for Managers. INSEAD Knowledge.

115 Impressive realistic Mark Zuckerberg avatar shown at Meta Connect. https://www.youtube.com/watch?v=So8GdQD0Qyc.

116 Video Gaming & eSports. *Statista*. https://www.statista.com/markets/417/topic/478/video-gaming-esports/#overview.

117 Koçak, Ö., & Puranam, P. (2022). Separated by a Common Language: How the Nature of Code Differences Shapes Communication Success and Code Convergence. *Management Science*, 68(7): 6287–6306. https://doi.org/10.1287/mnsc.2021.4157.

118 Koçak, Ö., Puranam, P., & Yegin, A. (2023). Decoding cultural conflicts. *Frontiers in Psychology*, 14, 166023.

119 Tinguely, P. N., Lee, J., & He, V. F. (2023). Designing Human Resource Management Systems in the Age of AI. *Journal of Organization Design*, 13.

120 Dastin, J. (2018). Insight - Amazon scraps secret AI recruiting tool that showed bias against women. *Reuters*. https://www.reuters.com/article/us-amazon-com-jobs-automation-insight/amazon-scraps-secret-ai-recruiting-tool-that-showed-bias-against-women-idUSKCN1MK08G/.

121 Puranam, P. (2019). Enlightened by Randomness. *INSEAD Knowledge*. https://knowledge.insead.edu/leadership-organisations/enlightened-randomness.

122 Neill, P. (2020). Revolutionising the commute is key to reducing $CO2$ emissions. *AirQualityNews*. https://airqualitynews.com/cars-freight-transport/revolutionising-the-commute-is-key-to-reducing-co2-emissions/

123 van Vugt, M., Colarelli, S. M., & Li, N. P. (2024). Digitally Connected, Evolutionarily Wired: An Evolutionary Mismatch Perspective on Digital Work. *Organizational Psychology Review*. https://doi.org/10.1177/20413866241232138.

Chapter 7: Digital (Non) Hierarchy

124 Written questions, answers, and statements. UK Parliament. https://questions-statements.parliament.uk/written-questions/detail/2020-02-12/1220.

The ratio falls to one supervisor for 8.3 prisoners in so called 'open' prisons where the inmates are generally non-violent and may even be allowed to periodically return home. It rises to one supervisor for every 1.6 prisoners in 'dispersal' prisons that house the most dangerous people, who might also be most likely to attempt escape.

125 Bentham's thinking is foundational for modern economics. His advocacy for the separation of church and state, equal rights for women, and individual freedoms have profoundly

affected the development of modern attitudes to these topics. You can view his preserved corpse—in a transparent glass case—at the University College of London (if you feel so inclined).

126 In this case, the threat of punishment by the vastly observant central actor is also suppressing conflicts from arising in the first place. It's an interesting exercise to compare the panopticon with the 'Leviathan' of Thomas Hobbes.

127 Zuboff, S. (2019). *The Age of Surveillance Capitalism: The Fight for a Human Future at the New Frontier of Power*. Profile Books.

128 Wulf, W. A. Improving Research Capabilities through Collaboratories. https://europepmc.org/books/n/nap9465/ddd00006/?extid=25077193&src=med.

129 Similar ideas have been described using terms such as heterarchy (McCulloch, W. S. [1945]. A heterarchy of values determined by the topology of nervous nets. *Bulletin of Mathematical Biophysics*, 7[2]: 89–93); adhocracy (Mintzberg, H. [1979]. *The Structuring of Organizations*. Prentice-Hall, Englewood Cliffs); teal (Laloux, F. [2014]. *Reinventing Organizations*. Nelson Parker); and humanocracy (Hamel, G., & Zanini, M. [2020]. *Humanocracy: Creating Organizations as Amazing as the People Inside Them*. Harvard Business Review Press).

I like Wulf's 'collaboratory' because it combines the themes of collective exploration, digital technologies, and self-managing groups.

130 The formal definition of a hierarchy requires transitive, acyclic asymmetric relationships. Transitivity is undefined unless there are at least three layers.

131 It is an open question as to when the loss of autonomy to one's peers is more acceptable than its usurpation by a superior. See the concept of 'concertive control' in Barker, J. R. (1993). Tightening the Iron Cage: Concertive Control in Self-Managing Teams. *Administrative Science Quarterly*, 38(3): 408–437.

132 Wrangham, R. W. (2019). *The Goodness Paradox: How Evolution Makes Us More and Less Violent.* New York: Pantheon Books.

133 Narayanan, J., Puranam, P., & Van Vugt, M. (2022). Human-Centric Organizing: A Perspective from Evolutionary Psychology. INSEAD Working Paper No. 2022/59/STR.

   Also see Christakis, N. (2019). *Blueprint: The Evolutionary Origins of a Good Society.* New York, NY Little, Brown Spark.

134 Ryan, R. M., and Deci, E. L. (2017). Self-determination theory: Basic psychological needs in motivation, development, and wellness. *The Guilford Press.* https://doi.org/10.1521/978.14625/28806.

135 Laloux, F. (2014). *Reinventing Organizations.* Brussels: Nelson Parker.

136 You might wonder about expertise differences as a basis for authority hierarchy. It is indeed better if I accept your advice if you know more than me, but the only reason to give you authority over me (so that I obey even if I do not agree with you) is if we cannot agree on who in fact is correct. In other words, the mere existence of differences in expertise is not sufficient to produce a hierarchy of authority; it is the difficulty of agreeing on who is more likely to be displaying superior expertise that makes authority necessary.

   See Conner, K. R., & Prahalad, C. K. (1996). A Resource-Based Theory of the Firm: Knowledge versus Opportunism. *Organization Science*, 7(5): 477–501.

137 In fact, beyond a certain number of layers, hierarchies may become *de facto* decentralized because those at the top layers can no longer exert any meaningful control on those at the bottom; the theatre of compliance might however continue. This is one more reason not to confuse centralization with hierarchy.

138 Puranam, P. (2018). *The Microstructure of Organizations*, Chapter 6, Oxford University Press.

139 Laloux, F. (2014). *Reinventing Organisations: A Guide to Creating Organisations Inspired by the Next Stage of Human Consciousness*. Nelson Parker.

Hamel, G., & Zanini, M. (2020). *Humanocracy: Creating Organizations as Amazing as the People Inside Them*. Harvard Business Review Press.

Foss, N. J., & Klein, P. G. (2022). *Why Managers Matter: The Perils of the Bossless Company*. Hachette.

Reitzig, M. (2022). *Get Better at Flatter*. Springer.

He, V. F., & Puranam, P. (2024). "Collaborative organizing without authority" in Snow & Fjeldstad (Eds.) *Designing Modern Organizations*. Cambridge University Press.

Hsieh, Y., Verne, J.P., Anderson, P., Lakhani, K. & Reitzig, M. (2018). Bitcoin and the rise of decentralized autonomous organizations. *Journal of Organization Design*, 7(14).

140 This is a series of case studies with commentaries I curated at the *Journal of Organization Design* with Dorthe Dojbak Hakkonson.

See Introduction | Journal of Organization Design (jorgdesign.net)

141 Gulati, P., Marchetti, A., & Puranam, P. (2023). Digital Collaboration Technologies and Managerial Intensity in U.S. Corporations: An Examination. INSEAD Working Paper No. 2023/53/STR.

142 Mintzberg, H. (1973). The Nature of Managerial Work. *Harvard Business Review*, 51(3): 49–61.

Edwards, R. (1979). *Contested Terrain: The Transformation of the Workplace in the Twentieth Century*. New York: Basic Books.

143 Kellogg, K. C., Valentine, M., & Christin, A. (2020). Algorithms at work: The new contested terrain of control. *The Academy of Management Annals*, 14(1): 366–41.

144 Noponen, N., Feshchenko, P., Auvinen, T., Luoma-aho, V., & Abrahamsson, P. (2023). Taylorism on Steroids or

Enabling Autonomy? A Systematic Review of Algorithmic Management. *Management Review Quarterly.*

145 Hedlund, G. (1986). The hypermodern MNC—A heterarchy? *Human Resource Management,* 25(1): 9–35.

    Stark, D. (2009). *The Sense of Dissonance: Accounts of Worth in Economic Life.* Princeton University Press.

146 Puranam, P. (2023). How Organisation Design Can Rescue the SDGs. INSEAD Knowledge. https://knowledge.insead.edu/responsibility/how-organisation-design-can-rescue-sdgs

Chapter 8: Democratizing Organization Design

147 Galbraith, J. R. (1973). *Designing Complex Organizations.* Reading, MA: Addison-Wesley.

    Peters, T., & Waterman, R. H. (1982). *In search of excellence.* Harper and Row.

    Burton, R. M., DeSanctis, G., & Obel, B. (2006). *Organizational Design: A Step-by-Step Approach.* Cambridge University Press.

    Nadler, D., & Tushman, M. (1980). A Model for Diagnosing Organizational Behavior. *Organizational Dynamics,* 9(2): 35–51.

148 Workiewicz, M., & Levinthal, D. A. (2018). When Two Bosses Are Better Than One: Nearly Decomposable Systems and Organizational Adaptation. *Organization Science,* 29(2): 207–224.

149 Simon, H.A. (1962). The Architecture of Complexity. *Proceedings of the American Philosophical Society,* 106(6): 467–482.

150 For an excellent account of central planning failures in city planning and agriculture, see James Scott's *Seeing Like a State* (2020) Yale University Press. Also see the work of J Stephen Lansing on Balinese water-temples and the effect of thoughtlessly imposed government mandates on disrupting

the ecological balance the temples helped to preserve. Lansing, J. S., & Cox, M. P. (2017). *Islands of Order: A Guide to Complexity Modeling for the Social Sciences.* Princeton Studies in Complexity: Princeton University Press.

151 Park, S., Gonzalez, C., & Puranam, P. (Forthcoming). Decision centralization and learning from experience in groups: separating context from aggregation effects, *Management Science.*

152 Ostrom, E. (2005). *Understanding Institutional Diversity.* Princeton, NJ: Princeton University Press.

153 Weick, K. E. (1977). Organization design: Organizations as self-designing systems. *Organizational Dynamics*, 6(2): 31–46. https://doi.org/10.1016/0090-2616(77)90044-4.

154 Sitter, L.U.D., Hertog, J.F.D., & Dankbaar, B. (1997). From Complex Organizations with Simple Jobs to Simple Organizations with Complex Jobs. *Human Relations*, 50: 497–534. https://doi.org/10.1023/A:1016987702271

155 Adler, P. S., & Borys, B. (1996). Two Types of Bureaucracy: Enabling and Coercive. *Administrative Science Quarterly*, 41(1): 61–89.

   Also see Ferreras, I., Battilana, J., & Méda, D. (2022). *Democratize Work: The Case for Reorganizing the Economy.* University of Chicago Press, for the case for democratizing organizations through enhanced worker participation as a means for organizations to pursue multiple goals besides profits (such as sustainability).

156 Authors who disagree on how sustainable or real are the trends on the flattening of hierarchies agree nonetheless that the era of the command-and-control hierarchy is over. Foss, N. J., & Klein, P. G. (2022). *Why Managers Matter: The Perils of the Bossless Company.* Hachette UK.

   Reitzig, M. (2022). *Get Better at Flatter.* Springer.

   Hamel, G., & Zanini, M. (2020). *Humanocracy: Creating Organizations as Amazing as the People Inside Them.* Harvard Business Review Press.